Stating the Case for Mindfulness

<u>FOREWORD</u>

Initially I was going to write a book 'Using Mindfulness for Depression'. I didn't because it occurred to me that it was far too limited. Mindfulness is not solely for those feeling depressed or downhearted, but its usefulness for and the way of doing so are the same, whether depressed or not.

Further, depression itself in our society scales from catatonia to sadness and is commonly linked with anxiety, but ... Mindfulness is not limited to this scale, however encompassing that scale may be. Mindfulness also has application for and will be invaluable to, those suffering from sadness, boredom, loss, frustration, dissatisfaction, which at some point or another applies to every single one of us.

Mindfulness also applies to happiness. It uncovers a happiness that has been there all the time, we just didn't pay any attention to it.

So having scrapped the original title, I contemplated the question of who is my audience; who am I writing to? Am I aiming this book at individuals, corporations or the health industry? Is this a self-help book aimed at the service user or a guide for the practitioners and clinicians? In corporate terms, is it for the employers or the employees?

By token of what Mindfulness actually is, it has to be all. Sorry Mr Publisher if I am breaking the mould here, but that is just the way Mindfulness is.

Hence I began to establish what I definitely do want to do with this book. One of those things is to attempt to halt the confines currently being placed on both the usefulness and applications of Mindfulness.

What do I mean by confines? Well, in Mental Healthcare, for example, Mindfulness is being cultured to suit a system. Clients, namely those it is considered to be useful to, are having to meet certain criteria, and its application, or how it is to be utilised, is being required to follow a protocol. What protocol? Whose protocol? Mindfulness has already been removed from its original protocol, the religious and ritualistic elements having been removed. And even in healthcare, when it suits, be it for research or logistical purposes, it appears the parameters and protocols may be changed.

I do understand the reasoning behind the structuring of therapies, the governance and quality benefits of uniformity, however I do feel strongly that when doing so, we need to ensure we are not missing or losing, the original point. Mindfulness is not theirs or ours to confine. In Mindfulness there is no right way, no wrong way because Mindfulness is directly about becoming aware of what is.

Gunaratana so eloquently articulated, "You cannot teach someone Mindfulness, you can only show them where to begin" (1). Mindfulness is experiential. Like walking, you have to do it. Like walking, you will have your own pace and your own gait. And also like walking, where that ability then takes you is unique; it is a journey and it is up to you.

So it does not matter if you are practitioner or patient, CEO or tea-boy, because the ability to do, and then ultimately, the ability to share, promote, encourage or coach the uses of Mindfulness come from use, practice and experience.

Of course this being a book, the reader must at least have the motivation and the capability to begin reading. I accept when someone is in a catatonic state this is unlikely to be the case. Then you, the person who IS reading this book, now you can help them initially, registered practitioner or not. You are allowed and you are able to share words and practices of wisdom and balm. I vehemently state – you are allowed!

So ultimately, the purpose of this book is to provide further knowledge and understanding; the practices encouraged to provided capability and wider application - an eternally growing sea of such I hasten to add. Mindfulness has a limitless number of uses and applications. And of course in turn these provide numerous benefits.

So my case is stated for this being both a self-help book and a book for practitioners or managers. Potentially we all fit into all categories.

Mindfulness removes categorisations. It removes the labels and boxes the first world so commonly uses. It says "Come, see. Now come, see again. Nothing is static, this time is different. One moment I am clinician, one moment I am patient; one moment I am happy, one moment I am sad; one day I am able, one day I am not". That is ok, this is life, and Mindfulness is as Jon Kabat-Zin declares 'the science of a meaningful life'. (2)

What is intended through this book is simplicity; something to the point and applicable; something that addresses what Mindfulness actually is, and how it can be utilised by all and why it should be. This is the true reason for Mindfulness in its original form.

So in effect, I am 'Stating the Case for Mindfulness'. In stating its case I have to tell you how it is beyond useful, how it is so simple, and how it is so natural for us to do. If you try for yourself, you will see for yourself. You will see truth. Not the truth of society, not the truth of some wise man, but the truth of each moment, without prejudice.

Notes for Use

Due to the wide audience this book has been written for, some terms may be unfamiliar to some readers. In order to enable smooth uninterrupted reading, explanations are not included in the text, but there is a Glossary of Terms at the end of the book.

There is also a Bibliography. I recommend reading from it. Each perspective is a new perspective. Each new perspective gained is a new truth.

NB - A Very Important Note

This book contains comparisons between Mindfulness and medication. Do not stop taking prescribed medications without talking to the relevant Health Professional first. By all means explore the other options you encounter, especially Mindfulness. I can assure you in most cases, your Health Professional will be extremely pleased you want to try something other than medication, be it to aid and abet or replace and will support you to do so. But there are patients and particular conditions that definitely do benefit from medication. Within Mental Healthcare there are legislative situations where someone may be required to continue medication programmes.

You are unique, your health professional knows your specific case. So I reiterate - Do not stop taking prescribed medications without talking to the relevant Health Professional first.

Some medications need to be ceased slowly, not just stopped. Do get the required information and advice concerning your own particular needs.

But do speak. In all cases, being involved with and understanding your treatments and how and why they work is helpful.

Contents

FOREWORD 4

The facts and figures 12

Suffering 19

Appropriate Suffering 27

Mindful Awareness...37

Mindfulness – The Background 45

Using Mindfulness? 53

Practising Mindfulness 58

Utilising Cues 63

Principles 68

Living-In-The-Moment...*68*

Acceptance *72*

Non-Judgement...*76*

Seeing Anew...*77*

Non-Striving...*79*

The Purposeful Placing of Attention.................................82

Meditation...90

The Practice 93

Walking Meditation 102

Three Minute Meditation 103

Mindful Reflection 104

A Relaxation Technique 107

Doing Things Mindfully..112

How Does Mindfulness Help?...117

Some Shared Experiences 120

Glossary of Terms..**124**

Bibliography **125**

About the Author **129**

Only when we accept what is, do we have a stable base from which to move.

The facts and figures

General Practitioners see thousands of people a day suffering from stress, depression, anxiety and related disorders. These people are treated primarily by GPs and continue their treatment in this primary care service. Due to the huge number of presenting cases relatively few are ever accepted into secondary specialist care, the Mental Health Service.

Stress, anxiety and depression are a familiar occurrence in every branch of healthcare. I have worked in surgical wards where it is commonplace to witness much slower recovery from surgery because the patient is feeling depressed or anxious. Their physical healing is noticeably impaired by low mood.

Depression and anxiety are a common presentation in stroke rehabilitation units, again their presence seriously impedes potential recovery.

As a diagnosed condition in its own right, 1 in 6 adults living in the UK will suffer from anxiety and depression (3).

That's a lot of people! The figures are rising.

That figure includes only those with a registered diagnosis. It is estimated that a third of people suffering depression and half of those suffering with anxiety disorders remain undiagnosed and untreated

(4).   Mixed anxiety and depression is the most common mental health problem in the UK.

According to the Department of Health report 'No Health without Mental Health', the health service costs of diagnosed depression alone in the UK in 2007 was £1.7 billion. This condition cost the country a further £5.8 billion in loss of earnings, £1.7 – £2.8 billion attributable to lower productivity and a further £9.9 – £12.4 billion in human costs.

That's a lot of money! The figures are rising.

Most low to moderate depressive conditions are treated with antidepressants prescribed by the GP. In the UK 40 million prescriptions for antidepressants were given by GPs during the year of 2012. (5; 6).

Many of us personally know of people who have been taking anti-depressants for years. Maybe you are one of those people. The majority still consider themselves to be depressed. Most carry on taking antidepressants, despite not feeling cured because they are worried that without them life will feel even worse.

But... all is not lost. It is the current intent of many of the Trusts that make up our British National Health Service (NHS), to incorporate evidence based practice into everyday practice. Mindfulness is one of these practices. It appears as a promoted evidence-based intervention time and again.

The National Institute for Health and Care Excellence (NICE), recognises and issues treatment guidelines for depression symptoms that fall below the diagnostic criteria set out by DSM V and ICD 10 as well as addressing the varying levels of diagnosed depression and anxiety.

NICE guidelines promote psychological treatments alongside the use of antidepressants, but sadly, despite attempts to promote psychological services through the launch of the IAPTS programme, they are still extremely difficult to access via the NHS.

Psychological therapies do have positive results in the treatment of Depression; this has been researched and recorded many times (7), however, in the UK our health service is still not routinely providing them. This situation though is changing.

As part of the IAPTS project, the primary care service 'Time to Talk' was launched, but became almost immediately oversubscribed. It is currently common to wait many weeks if not months to gain access to this service, culminating in the result that many individuals are not being referred to it at all.

Consequently, self-help is not just becoming popular, it is becoming imperative. Self-help is also promoted by NICE.

It is worth knowing what research shows. The NICE recommended treatment of anxiety is set out in 3 stages; Stage 1. Education and self-help resources; Stage 2 self-help and psychological interventions. Only when stages 1 and 2 have not worked, does NICE recommend the use of medication (8). Regrettably, in the majority of cases, medication is the sole treatment because these psychological treatments are not readily available. Sadly medication alone rarely works as a cure.

As with depression, the first line medication recommended for GAD are anti-depressants. Periodically patients are still prescribed Benzodiazepines.

Benzodiazepines are classified as anti-anxiolytics and are licensed for the treatment of anxiety but only in the very short term. Ideally, short term should mean that if someone is absolutely hysterical and beyond the point of being calmed or calming themselves, then a benzodiazepine medication would be ideal; one or two, the short term. What often happens is benzodiazepines are prescribed in packs albeit for no more than two weeks as recommended, but then patients take them for two weeks and then simply request repeat prescriptions.

In acute inpatient services, benzodiazepines are routinely written up as PRN, (Latin *'Pro re nata')* meaning to be given as required). Because this has been the practice for many years in the Mental Health Service, many staff commonly use them as a first line intervention for anxiety, and often for comparatively mild agitation. In fact their use has become so normal and usual, that patients literally ask for them, believing the 'when required' equates to 'when I want one'. This is understandably so as the patient immediately recognises and is very grateful for the relief provided by that first benzodiazepine tablet. It is effective and it is easy.

Big but coming now - the perceived benefits are short lived. Very soon higher doses are required to produce the same effect. A dependency or addiction builds extremely quickly. The consequences of long term benzodiazepine use are often worse than the original symptoms they were prescribed for (9). People who have been using benzodiazepines daily for four weeks or more are advised to see their GPs and come off them slowly (10).

Medication for mood has been the subject of much criticism over the years. As far back as the 1950s Thomas Szasz, a Professor of Psychiatry himself, fiercely challenged the use of medication for what he termed to be issues of personal conduct (11). "The history of psychopharmacology, [that is the study of the effect of drugs on behaviour and mental activity], is littered with burnt-out volcanoes" stated Edward Shorter in his book 'Before Prozac' (12). More recently, Dr Joanna Moncrieff, herself a practising psychiatrist has added research, papers and books challenging the use of anti-depressants and other mental health medications with powerful force (13).

Neither anti-depressants nor benzodiazepines do anything to address the triggers of depression and anxiety. Unless the cause is totally due to chemical imbalance, the root of the problem remains unaddressed.

How do we know if chemical imbalance is the cause? To date there is no way to test levels of chemical messengers present in the nervous system of a live human being. Even posthumous research is difficult to verify as it is rare to find a subject that has received a diagnosis whilst living, but who has not been treated with psychiatric medications.

Common triggers for depression and anxiety include but are not exclusive to: bereavement, a divorce or difficult living circumstances, dissatisfaction, work pressures, relationship problems, financial difficulties, over work, boredom. The cause can also be habitual negative thinking habits, habitual worrying, or the inability of the sufferer to put life events into manageable perspectives. The cause could also be bad diet and lack of exercise. Basically common triggers and causes of depression and anxiety are everyday life.

Addressing these causes requires more than a pill. Psychological interventions educate patients about themselves. They show how you think and behave and then provide you with ways to change or replace ineffective or self-sabotaging thought patterns and subsequent self-sabotaging behaviours.

Mindfulness is a psychological intervention. Mindfulness is about becoming aware of yourself, without judgement and with acceptance. It is about learning to be able to watch, to inquire, to investigate, to know yourself in your own varying surroundings, but not becoming caught up mentally or emotionally with that enquiry.

In these days where 'money talks', it is of paramount relevance also that psychological treatments do have financial benefits. The Kings Fund report 'Paying the

Price' concluded that evidence-based psychological interventions not only had proven therapeutic effect, but also had the potential to reduce healthcare costs in quantities of billions of pounds (4).

There are also the commercial costs; absence time, non-productivity, low morale in the workplace. So Mindfulness is having a positive financial knock-on effect in the world of commerce (14). There is every reason for the world of business to sit up and take notice. Mindfulness in the Workplace is catching on fast.

Due primarily to the work of Jon Kabat-Zin, Mindfulness is a mainstream psychological therapy. However, Mindfulness application is not confined to mental healthcare; it is now regularly used in pain clinics, and is spreading across a range of physical health sectors.

Outside of healthcare, Mindfulness is rapidly becoming a part of modern day business practice; large corporate enterprises are employing the services of Mindful experts in an attempt to improve staff wellbeing, which of course is also an attempt to improve staff productivity - the two are inextricably linked.

Suffering

It is pertinent to ask the question – "are you depressed or are you unhappy?"

Is there a difference? Is being depressed different to being unhappy?

In acute inpatient mental health units we do see people in a catatonic state. These people are on the verge of dying, sometimes not even having the motivation to even open their eyes anymore, let alone eat or drink. These people are obviously extremely and severely clinically depressed. Administering medication in the form of antidepressants to these patients is often difficult but they do help, noticeably. Other treatments such as ECT also produce remarkable and indeed life-saving results [15].

Staging down, we also see (more) people who are clinically depressed and who do meet the criteria for a moderate to severe depression diagnosis in accordance with DSM V or ICD 10.

Coming further down the severity scale, we see people with depression, stress and anxiety classified as low to moderate, but which nevertheless is affecting their own life and the lives of those around them to an unacceptably detrimental extent. They are suffering.

In my experience there is nearly always an underlying reason fuelling this latter condition;

nearly always a circumstance they cannot or do not want to address.

And we see people who are simply unhappy, yes, even in an inpatient unit. These people are always unhappy for a genuine and valid reason, and are able to express this reason. However, in my experience, anti-depressants rarely help this group to a noticeable point. My own observations are echoed by research. A Meta-Data Analysis of data provided to the FDA for the licensing of four new-generation antidepressants, concluded that anti-depressants only had conclusive positive results on the groups suffering severe depressive states (6). Any positive effects from antidepressants on low to moderately depressed groups were negligible and comparable to control groups given placebos. More research, facts and figures supporting this conclusion can be found on the aforementioned website of Dr Joanna Moncrieff (13).

So there has to be a discernible difference between being depressed and being unhappy. Should being unhappy be pharmacologically treated? Is being unhappy the same as being ill? Szasz may have been controversial, but he certainly did make a lot of people sit up and notice and debate the benefit of medicalising human emotion (11).

Anxiety is definitely a natural phenomenon. It is physiological as well as mental and emotional and what's more, the fight/flight response is manifest throughout nature and for good reason (16).

Does it matter? Whether depressed or unhappy these people are all without doubt suffering. Suffering is suffering be it at the stage of miserable or on deaths door, be it chemically or socially induced, it is still suffering. So does it matter if there is a difference between being unhappy and being medically depressed?

Shorter was adamant that yes it does, because the importance, the relevance lay in the area of treatment (12). There is a difference between being unhappy for a valid or even invalid reason and being ill because each requires a different approach and a different solution. The treatment of severe clinical depression SHOULD be different from the treatment of unhappiness. In reality sadly, in a lot of cases, it isn't. On many occasions people are not distinguishing between depression and unhappiness anymore, be they clinicians or patients. The effect as we have discussed earlier is a lot of people taking a lot of tablets with no beneficial effect.

We have become a society that does not expect to suffer. And in the main, we tend to reach out to something outside of our-self to ease that suffering; in the main, in the Western World, that something is medication; in the main, our Health System obliges.

This book is not written to beat up our National Health Service. Heaven knows it is beat up enough. Our National Health Service does what it can within the confines of legislation, finance and logistics. It is often forgotten that what we call the NHS is a system of theories, policies and guidelines, run by corporate businesses, financed by pharmaceutical companies, but worked by individual hard working professionals, the majority of which actually do care and do their individual and team bests for patients with the options and resources available to them.

However, I can vouch for the fact that options and choices open to clinicians often feel like a choice between the proverbial devil and the deep blue sea. What a lot of clinical professionals are capable of doing and would like to do, is not an option within the confines of the NHS. There simply are not the resources or the opportunities or the time.

This provides us with a brilliant illustration showing why it is good to discern whether or not we are clinically depressed or terribly unhappy:-

Many of us professionals are unhappy about the limitations of the system, but would giving us all anti-depressants actually help?

The answer may be that for some who have excessive serotonin reuptake, antidepressants may indeed lift their mood and hence they wouldn't feel quite so bad when pondering it. But for the majority antidepressants wouldn't change a thing; taking antidepressants would not change an external circumstance that is highly frustrating and sometimes heart-breaking. That is the relevant point.

I seriously urge you to think about this if you or someone you know has been taking antidepressants but doesn't appear to be any better. Is there a reason the drugs don't work? Instead of feeling even more dismayed, dejected and let down because the drugs don't meet your expectations, ask yourself if you or they are seeking a solution from the wrong source.

This is not a case of stating medication is wrong - it is more a metaphorical question - 'Are you climbing round an apple tree trying to find a pear?' It is asking if medication alone is providing you with the solution you want and expect.

Being sad or unhappy isn't necessarily any less awful than being depressed or anxious. It feels terrible. It feels like you can't do it anymore, whatever 'it' may be. It taints the good in everything. It makes you want to curl up and hide. It makes you angry and irritable. It affects your eating, sleeping and concentration. It detrimentally affects your interactions with others and your own physical and mental wellbeing.

The issue I am highlighting is not the level of suffering, but differentiating the approach used to treat different kinds of suffering.

If we do not make this differentiation, it is tantamount to treating a broken leg with paracetamol. Paracetamol may temporarily ease some of the pain, but it won't fix the leg. Likewise, if someone is unhappy, raising their available serotonin or noradrenaline levels may make them feel slightly more functional, but it won't solve the root of the problem. If the problem remains the symptoms will remain and in some cases may worsen as the cause of the problem continues.

Suffering is not always a medical condition that needs treating with medicine. Furthermore incorrect treatments can actually prolong and/or exacerbate these conditions. Because of the developmental processes involved, what we refer to as appropriate sadness, unhappiness or stress, may well evolve into a higher severity of suffering if treated incorrectly.

A major reason this occurs is because of the expectation people have of the medication. When this expectation isn't met, when the drugs don't make them feel any better, disappointment, hopelessness and frustration are added to their already negative mix of emotion and thought.

Emotions have substantiated mental and physiological effects. Negative emotions have phenomenally negative and unfavourable mental and physical effects (17).

We have become a nation of 'I want it and I want it now'. We don't expect to suffer and we don't expect to be required to initiate change. We do go for what appears on the surface to be the easiest and quickest solution. So often it is all too easy to reach for a pill, expecting it to be the quickest and easiest cure-all.

However, let's look at this logically, let us become aware of the facts. If you want fast, the first thing to understand is that antidepressants aren't quick, they don't work NOW. They take time, and they initiate a subtle change. The majority of people expect that after two days of taking anti-depressants they are going to wake up happy. This does not happen. Anti-depressants are not the equivalent of happy pills. They have a delicate effect, one you are more likely to notice in retrospect.

In the cases of low to moderate depressive and anxious states, research is acknowledging that often the antidepressant drugs don't work at all, in that they have no noticeable, verifiable effect on the patients' mental wellbeing (6). Could this be because there was nothing wrong with their chemical messenger levels in the first place?

These questions have to be asked, and the answers need to be searched for. Mindfulness is awareness; that search for the truth that is, and acceptance of that truth without judgement. In Mindfulness there is no resistance to what is, neither is there any clinging to what is. Mindfulness is simply getting to know 'what is', without judgement, without preconception and without expectation.

Mindfulness promotes we sit in the now, place our attention on what is now; see it, get to know it. Now, this moment, includes us, me, you. It is our own unique experience within that we are becoming aware of.

Can you be honest with yourself? Deep down do you know the reason you aren't feeling happy? A lot of the time we don't know. We may list a hundred reasons why we aren't happy, but then we acknowledge those things still exist in moments when we do feel happy, however short-lived that may be. So a lot of the time we are left feeling an uncertainty, a doubt. We have un-nameable expectations of this thing called life and feel like we undertake a never ending search for sustainable happiness.

The magic begins when as we do become truthfully aware, we begin to realise that now is very different to how we have been thinking it is.

So where do we start?

Simply put, we start now with now. We start from whatever point we are at. As Hicks says so eloquently, wherever we put our boat in the river is where we are on the river. It may be in the middle of a divorce, it may be in the middle of a new adventure, it may be a time of tragedy or a time of euphoria (18). Whatever now is, now is and that is where we start.

Only when we really and honestly know and accept what is, do we have a stable base from which to move.

This statement will come up again and again throughout this book.

So let's look at the facts; let's acknowledge what is. Whether we want to hear it or not, 'it is'.

It is so important I make no apology for the repetition

Only when we really and honestly know and accept what is, do we have a stable base from which to move.

Appropriate Suffering

"The essence of life is suffering, said the Buddha." (1)

We mentioned earlier that as a society, we do not expect to have to suffer. We get a headache, we take a pill. We get indigestion, we take a medicine. We rarely stop to consider the cause of the headache, let alone a long term remedy, and likewise with the indigestion or reflux. We don't want to suffer, we have an expectation that we don't need to suffer: but as a society we are suffering greatly and despite the amount of pills we are consuming, the sufferings continue.

However, don't beat yourself up about this, accept it with compassion. It is a cultural thing; we have grown into a way of life, and we accept with a sense of expectation, there has to be a remedial pill. We place this expectation at the feet of our healthcare system and presume our expectations will be met. We are used to wellbeing solutions to be given to us, when we ourselves have not looked after our own system; we expect others can help when we simply do not look after ourselves.

As a nation we commonly smoke, drink, eat too much or too little of the right stuff. We commonly don't maintain our own physical wellbeing, let alone our mental state. We presume that if we 'contract something', there will be a treatment for it, which of course in the main there is.

However we are now beginning to realise that in many cases, pills are not the answer. In many cases of depression, anxiety and stress, pills are definitely NOT the singular answer. Medication can all too easily become a crutch the sufferer ends up identifying as a leg; feeling they can't live without it even though it is not producing the required result (4).

So with all the talk of suffering, let's start with suffering. Have you ever considered that sometimes, suffering may be appropriate?

What does that mean? How can suffering be appropriate?

Let's begin by looking at pain. We will start with a physical pain. If you put your hand in a flame, you will feel pain. It is normal for you to feel pain, it is appropriate for you to feel pain as it stops you from keeping your hand in the flame. To keep your hand in the flame would harm you. So in this example pain is the body's way of saying "don't keep doing this as it will harm you." That is appropriate.

Pain can continue after the event, so for example, even when you have removed your hand from the flame, you will still feel pain. This pain again is appropriate pain; it is usual and normal. Your hand is damaged, the skin is burnt, and the pain will make you protect your hand whilst it is wounded and vulnerable.

As another example, if you break an arm or sprain an ankle, that part of the body will hurt if you move it.

The pain you feel is beneficial in that it encourages you not to move it. The reason for this is that moving interferes with the healing process. Again, this is appropriate pain. Whilst unpleasant it is meant to be that way.

Of course, you can take some painkillers whilst the affected body part heals. I am not for one minute suggesting we need to suffer needlessly. I certainly do not advocate suffering if you don't need to and the point of this book is to share a practice that decreases our suffering momentously. There is a 'but', however. The 'but' is linked to our acceptance statement – *only when we know and accept what is do we have a stable base from which to move.*

Let's examine that statement in this context. What is it saying? Firstly, know and accept you have a damaged body part. Know and accept that painkillers are killing the pain, not curing the burn or the break. Do know and accept also the painkillers may cause you to forget your body part is damaged, and consequently you may not protect it as well as you otherwise would have. We have all experienced that, forgotten temporarily about the proverbial damaged hand and gone to grab something. Ouch! In some instances, the painkillers assist healing. Anti-inflammatory medication often does. So tablets aren't good or bad. We are not trying to judge, categorise or label. We are trying to become aware of all that is.

What about the headache? Very frequently our headaches are due to the fact that we rush around, don't drink enough and consequently we become dehydrated. When blood volume drops, the blood vessels in the head dilate to regulate the amount of oxygen reaching the brain. This and the chemical composition changes are translated by the brain as a headache. That headache is one of the ways our attention is being brought to the fact we are becoming dehydrated. What do we do? Frequently we take a painkiller and carry on, - so easy. Or is it? Taking a painkiller for dehydration really isn't very helpful at all. Did you know that even mild dehydration can affect your mood? (19). It would be more helpful and effective in the long term, if we address the cause of the dehydration and ensure we drink enough. If we ignore the early signs of dehydration, we will get more serious ones. We will eventually be forced to acknowledge the cause and most likely have damaged ourselves somewhat in the process because we didn't pay attention; we 'masked' the signals before getting to know and accepting what in reality was actually occurring. It is not the taking of the painkiller that is the problem, it is the masking of the problem; the 'not getting to know what is' first.

So knowing and accepting what really is, really does provide a stable base from which to move.

How about the reflux or indigestion? What may have caused that? Very often it is due to eating too quickly or eating whilst on the go. Alternatively, some NSAID's can cause reflux indigestion, so the cause could be the tablets you took for the headache!   Obesity can contribute to reflux indigestion when the weight forces the stomach acids back up the oesophageal tubes.   And sometimes there may be a serious cause that does require pharmacological intervention, but not in the form of antacids!

Whatever the reason, the quick fix of antacids doesn't address the cause, it masks it.   You were feeling uncomfortable for a reason.   Most pain or discomfort (suffering) is appropriate in that your brain is realising that something is wrong and it is attempting to make you, your conscious self, aware. It is fair to say your own system is expecting you to take notice, not to simply shut it up.

Moving onto emotional pain - If we lose a loved one, we suffer, we cry.   We are dreadfully unhappy; we feel emotional pain.   This is appropriate.   This is a normal human reaction and it does not mean the amount of serotonin reabsorbed by your nerve endings is excessive. It does not mean you are ill. It does not mean you are depressed in the sense you require antidepressants.   You are having a normal human reaction; you are not mentally unwell. You are however mentally and emotionally suffering.   It feels like your life has been damaged.   The pain is making you aware of that. It needs adjustment, it needs you to acknowledge change, it needs you to accept and be aware of the inevitility of everything.   A serious depression could be triggered by the loss of a loved one though.   Some people never get over it.   This really means they never adjust, so time does not heal the pain; they fail to recover. Do anti-depressants help in this case? I am sure the increase in available serotonin or noradrenaline isn't going to hinder anything, they may help. But I doubt anti-depressants alone will enable that person to make the necessary life adjustments, or help them turn grieving into pleasant remembering. It is a change in mental perspective that does that. A bereavement counsellor is going to have so much more chance of achieving long term benefits than anti-depressants will. Most definitely the anti-depressants will not stop that person feeling the initial grief, that pain, that suffering. They are not emotional pain killers. Anti-depressants will definitely not stop them missing that person. It is an appropriate human response to the loss of a loved one. The suffering is appropriate. The same applies to a relationship ceasing in any other way - It hurts, it really does, it is suffering. It requires you take notice and effect change.

I reiterate, I am not promoting suffering needlessly, I am illustrating that it has become all too easy to pop a pill before 'getting to know the pain'.

If you take the time to bring your awareness to it, to think about, to ponder the potential causes and initially accepting without judgement or resistance what is, you will provide yourself with a stable accurate base from which to move. It is more likely you will effect a helpful remedy.

Becoming aware of something means getting to know about it. Becoming aware is not altering it nor is it controlling it in any way. It is not expecting, clinging to or running from. Getting to know 'what is' is simply investigative. It provides surety, more factuality, more relevant information. In turn that means your next step, your next thought, action or behaviour, namely your response, in the next moment, is likely to be more pertinent, helpful and stable than if you are carrying out inattentive and hasty knee jerk reactions that have not taken into consideration what actually exists first.

With mental and emotional pain, all too often we do not accept how we really feel. This is perhaps because we believe we should not feel that particular way. Maybe we 'expect more' of ourselves. Maybe our pride is too delicate to accept we are hurting over something or someone. Maybe our ego has a problem admitting we feel down or lonely or sad or may have acted unhelpfully. Maybe we feel an emotion that isn't in keeping with our perceived expectations or demands of our friends, colleagues or family and hence we couldn't possibly accept we are feeling that way ourselves.

Sometimes, we actually, albeit subconsciously, hold onto pain. Illness, pain, suffering sometime elicits caring from others. If we are in a fragile emotional or mental state, sometimes our bodies display physical symptoms in response to our brains conveying there is a need for caring right now. Imagine how you may feel discovering that. Your ego may definitely reject that as the source of your suffering. Yet, if it is so, if that is the case here and now, also imagine all the suffering that will cease to continue if you become aware of that and can accept it without judgement.

I like to use an analogy to explain the effects of not acknowledging where you are at, of not acknowledging how you really do think or feel. If you are standing on a trampoline, but feel you shouldn't be for whatever reason, and try to ignore that fact, and consequently kid yourself you are on terra firm, your next step will be unstable. Stepping on a trampoline requires a very different approach than stepping on firm ground. If you do step on a trampoline in the same manner you step on solid ground, you will undoubtedly stumble, quite likely you will end up on your face rather than your feet. The same principle applies to your next steps in real life. If you do not without judgement acknowledge and accept the state you are in, acknowledge your feelings, your thoughts, your behaviours, and instead attempt to move from where you think you should be or want to be, rather than from where you actually are, that next step is likely to be unstable and unhelpful in real terms.

All too often, as we saw earlier with the headache or the reflux, we do not get to know what is really going on, we do not pay attention on purpose, so we never really become aware of what exactly it is our mind, our body or our heart is actually trying to tell us. And we carry on suffering, and so do those around us, and the pills don't work.

Acknowledging without prejudice, without altering; developing an awareness of what actually is, provides a sure, accurate base from which to move. Acknowledging our own existence, all of it, as it really is in this moment, provides surety and a huge amount of choice.

As we go through the book, you will come to know that aware is a more comfortable place to be. It gives us real choice. Complete awareness also enables safety. Further, as we stated earlier, we will begin to see that awareness of myself in the now, actually proves to be very different to what I have been thinking it is.

It is awareness with attitudes that promote complete truth not partial truth. It is awareness with compassion, non-judgement and acceptance of the nature of life. And with that awareness we begin to really see the root of the problems. We begin to see that our life as we have been experiencing it is based on thought not on fact. As Gunaratana so eloquently states, we get rid of the illusions and we begin to see with clarity (1). We start to understand exactly where the initial suffering comes from.

"The essence of life is suffering, said the Buddha." (1)

What does this mean?

Everything in the physical world will come forth, bloom and decay. Change will occur, it is inevitable. However much we want to hold onto a moment or a thing or a feeling, we can't. However much we want to avoid a moment or a thing or a feeling, we can't.

This inability to hold onto something we label as good and the inability to avoid something we label as bad, is the suffering the Buddha was referring to.

The Pali and Sanskrit word that we have translated into English as suffering is 'dukkha'.

Dukkha does not necessarily refer to suffering in the physical sense. It denotes suffering in terms of dissatisfaction, discontentment or unease. That ceaseless dissatisfaction around the fact that every moment disintegrates into the next. The Buddhists identified it as 'the human condition' and realised it came from the way in which we commonly view existence.

As humans we view life through our own lens and we judge experiences as good, bad or indifferent. I would like to substitute the word indifferent for OK. OK holds clearer daily meaning of the point to us British, we use it a lot. "I am ok", we say, rather than 'I am indifferent'.

Ok is ok; it is neither here nor there, largely we are not that bothered by it either way and more importantly we rarely bother with it.

So, our perceived existence, our experience of life, becomes constructed of what we classify to be good times that we attempt to cling onto or to find, that relentless searching, and the bad times which we attempt to avoid and persistently worry about even when they are not occurring. That bit in the middle, the ok bit, we rarely even register. We then further translate these thoughts, because that is what they are, just thoughts, into our emotional existential state.

Did you realise that mainly your experience of life is based on your thoughts. Your experience is rarely based in the reality of this moment. You have a thought about something you mentally label as good, and then your emotions follow. So does your body. You smile. You feel positive, happy. It's not here that thing. It's a thought. Alternatively, you have a worry or a concern. It's in your head currently, it is a thought, but your emotions follow. You experience fear or apprehension. Your physiology follows. Your stomach knots up. Your mouth downturns and your brows lower. In this moment it is a thought. If you are worrying about something happening, it is not happening now. If it was you would be dealing with it, not worrying about it, because it would be here and you would be in it, now. Yet you are experiencing that thought and you are experiencing it with emotion and body movement as if it were happening now.

Examples of these thought patterns that make up our experience of life now are - 'I cannot find a good partner, therefore I am unhappy.' 'I am bored or stressed with my job, therefore I am unhappy.' 'I will be happy when I win the lottery.' 'I would be happier if I did not have so much to do'. 'People expect too much with too little in return therefore I am feeling miserable'. Etc., etc.

Our minds natter on and on and on. It's a torrent of judgements, a free flow of preconceptions, a wild horse without reigns. Thought upon thought, upon thought. And where our thoughts go, our emotions follow. And where our emotions go gets displayed by our physiology. And that we interpret as life. Literally.

This habit of ours is a relentless albeit pointless exercise. We attach mental labels and judgements and preconceptions to everything and then we either cling on or we resist. We have thoughts, just thoughts, but these thoughts control our emotions. Our thoughts make us 'feel' the way they are thinking, namely, good, bad or ok.

This is the suffering 'dukkha' is conveying. It is dissatisfaction. It is that gnawing in the background. It is that relentless striving for something we never quite reach. It is the quick disintegration of the happiness that we thought would stay. We are continuously thinking in terms of good and bad and continuously trying to grab hold of, or to keep away from, and the truth is we can't. And that can't causes suffering – dukkha.

Mindful Awareness

Next steps are inevitable, we never stay where we are.

Suffering is the same, it also ebbs and flows – this is life; nothing remains the same from one moment to the next.

Mindfulness is asking us to notice this, to inquire into our real existence in this very moment here and now and to experience that instead of experiencing our thought. It is inviting us to become aware of THIS moment; to see it, feel it, taste it, smell it, and hear it, this moment now.

In the very next moment this moment has gone, it has become another moment with something different about it or in it, and truth was we missed it; we missed so many truths, so many moments, because we were experiencing our thoughts.

Think about it – if we really experience each and every moment, keep our awareness in this moment, how different would our experience of life be?

Try it now. How is this moment now for you? Are you cold, warm? Are you comfortable? Are you thirsty, hungry? What is around you? Is there a smell or a sound that you hadn't noticed until you placed your attention on this moment?

If we bring our awareness to this moment and explore it, really get to know it, the place we are really at now, we begin to experience life very differently. And further, because we have given this moment attention and developed an awareness of it, we actually know it for what it really is. And what this moment is actually made up of is vast – so very vast. There are so many things about this moment if you begin to notice them. From that we then realise we live in a universe full of choice, from each moment to the next. And because we have come to know that part of that moment we are really in, we begin to take stable steps instead of carrying out automatic responses without really thinking.

However, we still cannot cling onto the good things this moment holds. We may feel good in any particular moment, but we accept we have absolutely no way of holding it there or guaranteeing it in the next moment. This moment disintegrates into the next moment as does the next and the next and the next. Nothing, absolutely nothing remains the same.

Acknowledging that is acceptance. It is accepting this moment is this moment and good bad or ok it will inevitably dissolve into the next moment – that simply is the nature of life. And all the worrying or all the clinging is not going to change that. Why try, why suffer that relentless suffering that trying brings. That kind of trying just brings inevitable disappointment, yet more suffering. So Mindful awareness has to be developed with that acceptance. This moment is this moment only and the next one is different.

How often have we chased something we felt to be good, then when we have it we find the happy feeling is short lived?   It's the old adage, would Christmas be good if it was Christmas every day? Good is comparative, good is not a fixed point on a scale, it moves.   So we also need to remove those labels, good, bad, ok.   Let's replace them with meaning, awareness of what is. Good, bad, they are simply measures, comparisons against something else. Change the something else and the comparison moves.   So it transpires we realise we are chasing something that is never static, we will never get there, simply because there is no there, there is only now.

So far, our adult existence, our experience of life now, has been largely governed by our thoughts. On reflection, there is very little actually occurring in any given moment that relates to those thoughts, or our perceived state of existence.   When we are chatting happily to a neighbour, whether or not we win the lottery next week bears no relevance to that moment, that conversation, that interaction.   If we feel sad having just watched a sad movie, finding a new partner is unlikely to change our emotion in that moment. In fact most of the time, our perceived state of being, namely, happy, sad or ok, is based on our thoughts, not on our reality.   Our emotional state is relative to the subject of our attention. And rarely is our attention ever placed, on purpose to our actual experience of this current moment.

Mindfulness addresses this. Mindfulness requires we pay attention to this moment, to what actually is in it now and to our experience of that which is happening now. Mindfulness practice actually requires we become aware of reality and free ourselves of the tormented existence of our thoughts, namely our worries, our desires, our expectations, our fears. These thoughts, these mental projections of a future that is yet to happen, or reminiscing of an event that has long since gone, they are not real, they are merely thoughts. Yet these thoughts are translated by us as 'my life', my existence.

Furthermore, the standards, the scale by which we tend to judge the quality of our own existence, namely, the good, bad or ok, these are relative concepts. They move. They depend on your point of view. They depend on what happened before. They are comparative to our own experience thus far, and our own perception of the experiences of those around us.

Let's enquire further - what is good? What does having a good experience actually mean? How is it good? Have you ever bothered to really look and see and feel and hear? What does good feel like? What actually is the experience? What effect does it have on your toes? When things are really good, do we explore what good feels like? Do we taste it, or smell it? Or do we mainly state it and then find the novelty has worn off already and we didn't really notice what it felt like. And now it is gone. That is 'Dukkha'.

Furthermore, do we in this moment begin to suspect this good feeling may go and begin to worry about losing it, or start stressing about how to keep it? Do we turn the wonderful experience that we are actually having right now, into a fear, a worry about what is not actually happening here and now? That is dukkha.

I guarantee you, that if you bring your awareness into the moment when something feels good, and you really get to know what feeling good actually feels like, you will appreciate that actually you are feeling good a lot more times than you realise.

What happens is we categorise events and situations that are good. Then we define '*good*' as being those situations or events. And when one of those categorised events or situations is not occurring in this moment, we pay no attention to what we actually feel. And when we are paying no attention and someone asks us how we feel, we reply with the adjective '*ok*'. The absence of one or more of those things we have labelled as '*good*' means this moment has fallen into the category of '*ok*' (provided of course there is not the presence of something we have labelled as '*bad*'). And because it has fallen into the category of ok, we pay no attention to this moment at all. Our attention goes elsewhere; on the shopping we have to buy later, on the holiday we are going on next month or on the argument we had with our partner or children this morning. And our emotional state becomes to do with what we are thinking, that upon which we are placing our attention. Our emotional state rarely bears relevance to what is actually happening in this moment, this one here and now.

Please do it now. Please observe how you feel now? How does that chair feel to you? Have you noticed before? How do those slippers or shoes feel on your feet? Are you comfortable? Are you cold? On the whole, don't you actually feel ok? Right here and now, of the things that are actually in this moment with you now, exactly now, is anything at all so bad?

If you are feeling low now, is it because of what you are doing or where you are now? Is reading this book depressing? Is the chair depressing you? Are you unhappy because you don't want to be here right now? If the latter is the case, I am going to presume there is a reason why you are still here right now. And I am going to ask you to place your attention on what being here now actually feels like. Not your thoughts, not your reminiscences of why you are here or your forecasts of what you will do about it. Simply place your attention on what right now actually, really feels like. Is the weather nice? There are a million and one things happening in your vicinity right at this moment, what are they?

As humans, we categorise, we label, we presume, we expect, which means we judge. We do it nearly all the time to most things without being aware we are doing it. On the whole, our existence, our perceived reality is merely preconceived, prejudged thoughts, mainly of the past or the future, rarely about now.

Each day our brain receives millions of signals, light waves, sound waves, chemical messages and electrical impulses. The majority of these messages never come into our realm of conscious awareness. Rather subconscious processes in our brains filter; our conscious minds becoming aware only of what our conditioned mind deems to be relevant. The tiny bits of information that come into our awareness are a tiny fraction of the complete reality of this moment (16).

What's more, this thought induced reality, we believe, is shared by others. If someone does not share our reality, it is common to think of them as 'strange' or even 'mad'. We judge. Because of the instincts we inherently have, our pack instinct will consider it useful to notice, to be aware of the same things the rest of our pack are aware of. We also automatically react to judgement or perceived judgement of ourselves. On one level or another it affects our existence in the pack. So we both judge and we react to judgement. This is one of our many filtering processes.

We label nearly everything and when we agree with each other's labels, we presume ourselves to be having the same experience and therefore we name it reality and accept it as such, believing it to be true.

However we may not be; there is no way to compare how I experience blue with how you experience blue.

We just both call it blue. Your experience of blue could be more similar to my experience of red, but the fact we have labelled our experience of that particular combination of light reflection and absorption the same name, we will presume we are having the same experience, and furthermore, conclude this must be real.

Another potent filter is our belief system. We rarely acknowledge awareness of anything that does not fit into our own belief system. Have you ever experienced something you question is real? It is likely that because you do not believe it could be real, in other words, because it does not fit into your own belief system, you have dismissed it. In addition to this dismissal from awareness, most of the things that do not fit into our belief system don't even make it into our awareness. Our subconscious dismissed them before we even noticed.

This is the basis of what we identify as reality. Yet underneath, we are aware of a contradiction and also we all get that uncomfortable feeling there is more. And because of that we remain in a state of unsatisfied mental and emotional searching. All of this is Dukkha, suffering.

We achieve what we label *'good'* and we seek to hold it in time, but we cannot. We are aware of pitfalls, of threats of loss, discomfort or pain and we try hard to avoid these, but we cannot. This is suffering. The human condition of believing thought and perception to be reality, and seeking to control it, this is suffering; this is dukkha.

Things happen despite our best efforts. Each moment passes to the next whether we want it to or not. Yourself, your environment, other people around you, everything changes as each moment passes yet we seek to hold onto or avoid. And that constant mental grabbing and avoiding is what takes our attention.

So how do we develop Mindful Awareness? How do we practice Mindfulness? How do we become Mindful?

Mindfulness – The Background

It is said that Buddha himself spoke the words "Come, See". That is the goal of Mindfulness – for each individual to 'come, see with the presence of heart' (1).

In many Asian languages, the words for mind and heart are the same. Mindfulness therefore may also be thought of as Heartfulness. The Chinese word '*Xin*' is also translated as both heart and mind.

I always feel there is more to this linguistic fact than us Westerners initially realise. There is a profound message here from ancient wisdom that is a major key or pointer to the essence of what we now term Mindfulness.

If they called heart and mind the same word, they thought of it as the same thing, or that the two things, heart and mind equalled the one thing - *Xin*. This is so relevant to understanding what we mean by awareness.

If I have my heart and mind attuned to one thing, I become really aware of it. That awareness is almost experiencing a presence, the presence and essence of that which I am placing my heart and mind attention on. Try it, see what you experience if you place your heart and mind onto something. Don't simply think it, feel it; place your heart and mind on it.

The awareness we are attempting to achieve, or re-achieve, as it is an awareness we were born with, is the entirety of knowing that comes when we not only think, but feel. It's about becoming aware of all the things that are occurring behind the ego, behind the conditioned conscious thinking that we westerners rely so heavily on. Mindfulness is about engaging our hearts, our full feeling senses and listening, seeing, smelling, hearing, getting to know for the very first time.

Mindfulness was the seventh step of the Path of Enlightenment as taught by Buddha; enlightenment being a state in which greed, hatred and delusion have been overcome, abandoned from the mind. This place, or this state was called Nirvana. The translation of *Nirvana* is *'blowing out'.* Nirvana was the state achieved when greed hatred and delusion had been blown out.

Greed, hatred and delusion are things that cause us suffering. We may not think of ourselves as greedy specifically, but what we term ambition is a form of greed. The fact that we are trying to line our own nests, hold onto the good times, 'get somewhere' in life, keep up with the neighbours; these are the grabbing, holding onto things we automatically do in life and this is, when you are able to accept without judgement, greed.

Of course we think of these things as necessary. In our society it feels as if they are, we are taught to strive for success. We are conditioned to expect that if we try hard we will achieve. In turn we expect that achievement to be recognised by our peers and out bosses and that in turn will result in pay rises and nice things. These things are not 'bad' or 'wrong', but they are a form of greed and do cause dis-ease, stress, dissatisfaction or another word that encompasses them all - 'suffering'.

Hatred – what a horrid feeling that is. I once heard hatred is a form of fear, a strong form of fear. When we feel hatred we feel agitated, unsettled, demonstrative and unhappy. That is suffering.

And illusion - we are beginning to realise that most of our existence is an illusion, because most of our perceived existence is just thoughts, most of how we perceive ourselves to be living is not what our life is actually like in each moment at all.

So what could initially be thought of as some religious or hermetical statement 'Free yourself from greed, hatred and delusion', begins to take on the real wisdom that was intended. And that wisdom is applies here and now very much in this 21st century.

Successful meditators are not pious figures clothed in sackcloth and sandals. They are successful, happy, people who are learning to utilise all of their senses, and realise things in life for what they really are (1). They are mastering the ability to disengage themselves from living or experiencing existence purely through the cultivated ego, and exist in a life of learning from each moment, experiencing each moment, with a sense of detachment, or as an observer. This detached observing allied with acceptance and compassion instead of judged and turned away from, enables ease, rather than dis-ease.

The word '*Mindfulness*' is translated from the Pali and latterly Sanskrit term '*smrti* ' which literally translates as '*of the memory*' or '*that which becomes remembered*' or '*awareness*'.

Total awareness requires allowing. You cannot be truly aware if you are unable to accept or receive into your awareness any part of that which is.

In order to accept something is as it is requires the ability to put aside judgement and expectation; to accept without filters of preconceptions, prerequisites or prejudices. Mindfulness allows it, to be exactly as 'it' is.

Mindfulness is often referred to as 'living in the moment'. It is the skill of bringing one's complete attention to one's present experience on a moment-to-moment basis, of becoming aware of present existence as it continues to play out.

It involves paying attention in a particular and purposeful way to the present moment (2). It requires you view all in the detached manner of the observer; enquiring of everything as if seeing for the first time and allowing it to be, just as it is.

Everything that arises in the attentional field is acknowledged and accepted in an exploratory manner. Awareness of and acceptance of the temporary existence of all, is the primary intention.

Mindfulness is a practice, a discipline and eventually, a way of life.

Becoming mindful widens our perspectives and increases our 'view'. This in turn reduces fear, which in turn reduces inner and outer conflict. This in turn increases peace of mind, satisfaction and enjoyment. Again in turn all this leads to wellbeing, physically, mentally and emotionally. It develops into an 'ease' of living. Now you see why we think of Nirvana as meaning peaceful bliss.

Mindfulness enables you to disentangle yourself from your thought processes. It is the mental art of stepping out of your own way. It is a practical skill that focuses on everyday events and has immediate application in everybody's life [1].

Mindfulness meditation develops concentration. Your ability to concentrate, to focus, to remember will improve. Your ability to function mentally increases substantially as you get out of your own way. Mindfulness meditation allows you access to all the knowledge you have deep in your subconscious. It shuts up the incessant natter and chatter of our own thoughts and lets information flow in and out of our conscious awareness. It is mental housekeeping.

It clears out all the irrelevant nonsense and garbage that blocks our own natural ability to think freely and clearly. Therefore the effectiveness of all your mental abilities increases.

Mindfulness also aids rest. It enables you to relax at will. Even your sleep will be more rejuvenating.

Mindfulness was first introduced as a psychological intervention for stress reduction by Jon Kabat-Zin in 1979. Kabat-Zin describes Mindfulness as the Science of a Meaningful Life [2]. He defines it as the art of paying attention on purpose, in a particular way, to the present moment; in other words – pure untarnished purposeful awareness of each moment as it really is, as opposed to how we were 'thinking' it to be.

Mindfulness Based Cognitive Therapy (MBCT) was then developed by Zindel Segal, Mark Williams and John Teasdale, based on Jon Kabat-Zinn's MBSR programme. The MBCT programme was designed specifically to help people who suffer repeated bouts of depression [20].

Due to the pioneering works of people like Jon Kabat-Zin, Mindfulness has become an evidence based practice now widely used throughout our British National Health Service.

Many of its principles and practices can be found in self-improvement programmes, motivational literatures and Management Training Programmes. Many commercial enterprises are beginning to adopt its practices and principles; Mindfulness in the Workplace is currently big news and spreading rapidly. Mindful Management is also highly topical.

Mindfulness practice has been successfully implemented into the world of psychology and therefore inevitably has strong links and applications to the art of management, as do other humanity related disciplines and practices such as Neuro Linguistic programming (NLP) and sociology.

Two major advantages of Mindful Management Practise (as all the above already applies) is 1) it is applied inwards and 2) it supports the wellbeing of not only those being managed, but of the manager him/herself. The benefit of having a discipline or practice that is applied inwards rather than outwards is it remains steadfast and consistently applicable despite forever changing external environments and circumstances.

The beauty of mutual wellbeing speaks for itself; anything that supports wellbeing does not need further justification. Wellbeing affects existence itself and therefore impacts on every human action and interaction, management, productivity, efficiency being just a few of these.

Mindfulness Based Stress Reduction (MBSR) and Mindfulness Based Cognitive Therapy (MBCT) are accepted therapeutic interventions throughout the Western World. Research studies may be found via the National Institute for Health and Care Excellence (NICE) website showing positive results in both the treatment and relapse prevention of stress, anxiety, depression, OCD, PTSD, substance misuse, pain management, blood pressure disorders, personality disorders and many more psychological, psychiatric and physical conditions including neurological and immune disorders and more recently, cancer (21).

It is also shown to have very positive effects on healthy subjects.

Using Mindfulness?

Below are some of the ways people have answered the question *'What Is Mindfulness?'*

"Bringing one's attention to the present experience on a moment by moment basis."

"Paying attention in the moment in a specific way, i.e. non-judgmentally."

"Present-centred awareness in which each thought, feeling, or sensation that arises in the attentional field is acknowledged and accepted as it is."

"Choosing a present moment awareness based on curiosity, openness, and acceptance."

We think we know things, we think we see, we think we are aware, but in actuality most of us live our lives cocooned in our own perceptions of a reality that isn't actually reality at all. The largest proportion of our daily existence goes unnoticed as we rush here and there, ruminating about a past event, and stressing about a future one. We chase our desires and attempt avoiding our fears. In truth both our desires and fears are mere thoughts that can neither be held onto nor avoided. (1)

Through Mindfulness, we can choose our perceptions, we can open our senses, and we can know ourselves without fear of self-reprisal. Inner conflict is allowed to become resolved. Inner conflict is nearly always the cause of anxiety.

Through Mindfulness we empower ourselves to see situations in wider and also different terms.

We will experience shifts in our viewpoints, our expectations and our priorities. We will enable ourselves to perceive any situation in many different ways (16).

This book is primarily written using the practices and principles of Mindfulness. However it also makes use of, and therefore makes useful, some techniques commonly used in Neuro Linguistic Programming (NLP) and Cognitive Behavioural Therapy (CBT). You will notice Mindfulness is used in many forms of therapy and self-development programmes.

It is important to realise from the start that the suggestions and illustrations used in this book, are just that – suggestions and illustrations. The whole point of this book is to give you an understanding, to know Mindfulness enough within your own conceptual realisation, that you, the reader can then apply Mindfulness to you, your life.

This book imparts the knowledge and understanding to a degree. It is your practice and application that fulfils its purpose. We previously used the analogy of learning to walk. I can tell you how to walk, but unless you get up and do it, nothing will happen. The same is so of Mindfulness.

Another thing with Mindfulness is, there is no wrong or right. In fact these two adjectives cease to have relevance to most things when Mindfulness is applied. Mindfulness literally is awareness of what is, without judgment.

What is, what exists, is a conceptual topic. Each person will 'see' differently. Reality for one is not the same as reality for another, and therefore the same applies to application. However Mindfulness is a concept and a practice so far removed from our current everyday way of mentally being, that guidance is needed to facilitate understanding. People really understand when they practice, so this book doesn't just say what Mindfulness is, it gives examples of how Mindfulness may be applied as a practice, a discipline, and how it may be applied to general everyday living.

However, YOU have to do the practice. I can tell you, someone else can show you, others may guide you, but YOU are the one who has to do it, for it to be of any benefit.

Anybody and everybody can benefit from the knowledge, examples and practices shared in this book. This is me communicating with you about everyday interactions in everyday life. I am merely sharing knowledge and experience. Think of all the little bits you gain towards your own practice as a jigsaw puzzle. This book will give you more pieces. You add it to your life jigsaw, your existing circumstances, your existing knowledge, your own existential experience of life and you have your very own picture.

The aim is that as you read, discuss or even study this book, your perceptions, your experiences, your life will become integrated into this reading experience by token of the fact it will all become relevant and applicable to you.

There are disciplines, there are things I invite you to participate in. Whether you participate, as well as how you participate, is totally your choice. This has to be the essential pre-statement about this particular journey, this particular experience for everyone – it is your choice. This is about showing you your options; choices that do already exist; choices that we commonly fail to miss in each and every moment. This is about you knowing you, you seeing all of your world, and you choosing both what and how you interact with in it. These are your individual decisions and know from stage one that they are only yours to make.

Don't read or study this book from the perspective of 'what I am going to do to someone else' or from the perspective of 'this is what she is saying'. Rather come from the perspective of 'I am reading this book to learn about me'. If you read this book whilst applying it yourself to yourself, it will give you that deeper understanding, that empathy, that connection, that AWARENESS. Mindfulness is not just a practice for the sick; it is both a preventative and a treatment. Most importantly it is therapeutic to life.

I have successfully used the applications and techniques discussed in Group Work, One to One

Sessions and in my own personal everyday life. In my own personal life I go through periods where I apply the disciplines regularly, with great effect. Sometimes I go through periods where I allow life's demands to take control again and I don't. Then I notice the signs of stress returning. It's as simple as that. Whether I am the victor or the victim, remains my choice. And life is as life is – we all go in and out of both states and many states and stages in-between. This is life - and there lies a great introduction to Mindfulness.

Practising Mindfulness

I mentioned in the foreword that one of my goals for this book is that it will enable all to utilise Mindfulness if they choose to do so. The level of utilisation will affect the level of benefits. However it is imperative we realise that Mindfulness is self-perpetuating.

The more you do it mindfully and heartfully, the more you want to do it.

Also, the more you do it, the more able to do it you become. Therein lies my argument against anyone ever stating that participants need to meet certain criteria.

It is my passionate belief that Mindfulness can start from anywhere. This is the basis from which Mindfulness emanates – acceptance of now, acceptance of what is, no prerequisites, now is just fine.

It needs to be noted that Mindfulness as a psychological intervention has originated from a disciplined Buddhist practice. The discipline of the initial Buddhist practice was intense and included rituals and religion. Most MBSR programmes require you practise meditations daily over an eight week period. This 'gives meditative practice a fair try' as so eloquently put by Kabat-Zin (2).

I urge you to initiate a meditation programme for yourself. In many practises the recommended time is a minimum of 30 minutes each day. There is a valid, viable reason for this. However, I am urging you to begin with what you are able, but with the application of self-discipline. The reason I urge this is that something is better than nothing. When you are practising alone, unguided, or if you are currently acutely unwell, to state you have to do 30 minutes or it won't work is incorrect. I remain an advocate of Mindfulness as a Nursing Approach, and I staunchly defend my stance. Many people in an acutely unwell state, genuinely cannot manage 45 minutes continuous meditation, however that should not exclude them and Mindfulness certainly does not exclude them.

When meditating, you are learning the ability to keep your attention on a specified point and you are increasing your mental ability to do this every time you meditate, be it for 5 minutes or 45. At each attempt you will become more proficient, that is the nature of the physiology of neurones (16). That is how neural networking works.

We think extremely quickly. When we regularly do something, we gain the ability to put that thought into effect extremely quickly.

A good example of this is driving. When we initially start learning to drive we are conscious of every movement we have to make; one foot on clutch, the other on accelerator, carefully bringing one foot up as the other goes down; hands on steering wheel, changing gear and indicating; looking forwards and glancing backwards through mirrors. At first we wonder how we will ever be able to accomplish all these different tasks at the same time and whilst moving!

However, as we practice, it becomes easier, and eventually, driving – doing this combination of tasks at once, becomes second nature, habit; we don't think about it anymore. Our mind accepts the information, integrates all the various processes, and becomes able to utilise this data in a very fast and complex way, enabling us to make potentially lifesaving decisions on busy motorways on the go as it happens, or 'in each moment'.

Likewise with Mindful Meditation, the more you practise placing your attention on purpose, acknowledging your mind wanders and returning your attention gently on purpose, the easier it becomes.

As Mindfulness Principles becomes a way of being, a regular practice, our minds utilise these principles in this same fast and efficient manner.

It is, without doubt, beneficial to be 'religious' about practice, or to give your practice a disciplined regularity. We do this with food and with sleep, in the same vein and for the same reasons. So if you can, it is best to practice Mindfulness in this way. Consider it as necessary to your wellbeing as food and sleep, give it commitment and regularity.

Viewing Mindfulness as we do food is a good analogy. When someone is not well, they may not be able to eat a whole meal, however the little bits they can eat do produce benefits. It is my belief and experience with Mindfulness that there is a benefit in doing what you can to begin with and building it up. Benefits start when you become aware of how you are actually living. It is my belief that you already have benefitted from Mindfulness, simply by getting this far in this book.

When I am with people who are experiencing an extreme episode of anxiety or agitation or mania, there is no way those persons are in a state of mind or body to do a 30 or 45 minute meditation session. They are however able to breathe. Three minutes of a nurse or a friend or a family member, calmly reminding them that here and now they are ok, that here and now they are safe, that here and now in this moment there is nothing to worry about; calmly guiding them to just breathe as their breath wants to breathe, and realise exactly how they are right now, does have in the moment benefits, mental, emotional and physical and it does help towards recovery.

When anxiety attacks, you can have a Mindful bath, a Mindful walk, or even simply sit and have a few Mindful moments.

As displayed in its applications in the business world, you can do almost anything 'Mindfully'. It does have indisputable benefits even at this level. In business these benefits include organisational ability, effectiveness, time management, productivity, all at the same time as individual wellbeing.

There are countless advantages and these will be unique to you. They will come in forms I could never dream up to tell you, because you are unique.

Having held groups and run courses, and used Mindfulness in one to one interventions, I have come across an array of ways that Mindfulness has improved the quality of life for various individuals. I will list some later as you will see how varied and unique they are.

Utilising Cues

Just as we automatically experience triggers, we may experience cues.

We have these cues when doing lots of things, again to use driving as an example, we always start the same way, maybe - key in ignition, turn, hear engine, glance in mirrors. This becomes our cue to drive – we automatically go into driving mode from that cue. Key, sound of engine, mirrors, we drive; we carry out all the different behaviours relevant to driving, without having to consciously think about each movement and task. Our minds are phenomenally fast.

Cues, or anchors are they are referred to in NLP (15), act in a similar way triggers do when they cause an anxiety attack.

The cause of anxiety attacks is coming into contact with or mentally experiencing a trigger, something you consciously or subconsciously relate with an experience in which you felt fear. This trigger activates the body's fight/flight response, causing palpitations, rapid breathing and knotted stomach, and of course the emotional feeling of fear. Because there is nothing appropriate to contribute a fight/flight response to, the fear subsequently is inappropriate to the situation, hence this is called an anxiety attack. Becoming aware of yourself and of your own reactions helps to identify triggers, which in turn helps you to manage anxiety attacks.

However, there is an opposite. We can utilise our own system here and purposefully bring about a different conditioned response to a particular stimuli. Would it surprise you to learn you can bring about a relaxed state? Cues, like triggers bring about a certain response. A relaxed state can become a conditioned response and it is not difficult.

You simply start every relaxation and every meditation in the same way. For example I always begin my own and group meditation and relaxation sessions by saying 'Let's take two slightly deeper than normal breaths', and then taking two slightly deeper than normal breaths. Because I do this every time, this has become a cue (trigger) to a relaxed state. Eventually your brain will associate that particular stimulus with whatever you are currently doing with it, in this case, a relaxation session cued by the initial two deep breaths.

Effectively, triggers, cues and anchors are all different terms for the same type of process, and furthermore, if we know we already have the ability to react to triggers for negative states, it follows we must have the ability to condition ourselves, to utilise anchors or cues, for positive states.

As said before, there are many different disciplines or interventions that utilise various aspects of Mindfulness. NLP and CBT are two that spring immediately to mind. In mental healthcare, Mindfulness has developed into two specific interventions, MBSR – Mindfulness Based Stress

Reduction and MBCT – Mindfulness Based Cognitive Therapy.

Cognitive Behavioural Therapy teaches us to identify and challenge habitual thinking habits and filters that effect habitual behaviours.

We are all habitual in the way we think. We discussed earlier some of the filters we automatically apply to our awareness. This is true of how we mentally view situations as well as things. If you do come across an upsetting situation, it is likely you will interpret it in an extremely habitual way.

An example of this is a common mental health assessment question we ask to gauge a person's self-esteem level. "If you are walking down the road, you see a neighbour, say hello, but she hurriedly rushes by without acknowledging you, what do you think?"

Often the reply of the subject denotes the perception or belief that the neighbour doesn't like him/her, or alternatively, they will begin to wonder if they have done something to offend the neighbour. In reality though, or in truth as we say in Mindful terms, it could be that the neighbour has just received some bad news, maybe a relative has been involved in an accident or something, or her work has asked her to come in urgently. Either way, in her haste, she is so busy thinking about getting to wherever quickly, or the things she has had to rush away from or to, that her attention is so engrossed she literally did not register the acknowledgement.

However, because it is habitual for that person with low self-esteem to think negatively of themselves, their automatic translation is 'they don't like me', or 'I have done something wrong'. And that is what they perceive and experience as reality.

Practising and applying Mindfulness breaks these thinking habits. It allows us to come to know ourselves, our reactions and our habits. It allows us to accept ourselves without judgement and with compassion and understanding. We don't beat ourselves up for being a certain way, thinking a certain way or behaving so, we simply become aware that we do. We accept it not as right or wrong, but just as 'is'.

If we wish to be mindful about this aspect of ourselves, we begin to understand the many potential reasons why we do what we do or think how we do. We also acknowledge the benefits these habits bring as well as the downfalls.

All we have to do is simply accept it is this in this moment. In doing so, the next time this may happen, we are automatically aware and we have further developed the capacity to 'see' from another perspective. We don't have to fight it. Thus we simply choose whether to think or act that way again. We have realised we have, many choices as to how we want to perceive any given situation and the ability to utilise those choices in real life situations, in the moment. We consequently then choose our next step in the next moment, but we do so from a sure and stable base, because we know and accept what exists in this moment, and that includes a multiple of reasons and loads of choices.

So you see even just applying Mindfulness principles or attitudes as they are often called can be beneficial. You can begin experiencing these benefits now simply by applying what you have read so far to situations as they arise.

Maximum benefit however is going to come from doing regular Mindful meditations. To still your nattering mind for a predetermined amount of time each day is as we have said before, is momentously beneficial. How and why is discussed later.

BUT, don't be put off from doing what you can here and now. If you manage to place your attention on purpose on your own breathing for five minutes twice a day, that will help you. Build it up as you can.

I would also strongly encourage you make it a daily practise beyond eight weeks. Mindfulness becomes a way of life. Benefits literally do compound and build. Likewise, if neglected, old habits creep back, as do old ways of missing each moment. Life is hectic and powerful and our mind is used to chattering away and narrating its own perception of it. I have practised Mindfulness for many years, but there are still periods in time where I don't. Those old habits of the mind return all too easily.

Mindfulness is never static. There is no point to be reached, as you will see. It continues, and I can also say again from experience, there is layer upon layer upon layer. As you get to grips with one element, you realise another layer. It truly is awesome when you practice.

I tend to think of Mindfulness as having two main components, namely the meditation exercises and the application of the principles (attitudes).

Principles

We have come across The Principles of Mindfulness already in this book. However, looking at them one by one helps gain further understanding.

It is enlightening when you use these principles, or as they are often called – attitudes, in daily life. As you do you will find your understanding of them becomes more profound and encompassing. You develop a deep awareness of them.

Mindfulness incorporates   the   principles   and practices of   Living-In-The- Moment, Acceptance, Non-Judgment, Seeing Anew, and Non-striving.

Living-In-The-Moment
In Mindfulness, the intention .is to bring your attention, your awareness into this moment. This causes you to live this moment and not be stuck in the past or anxious over the future.

Living in the Moment enables us to manage worries and stressors. Worries are nearly always based in the future. To help understand this, I like to retell a story of the man who was afraid of heights (22).

After many years of putting it off, this man finally agreed to take his wife and son on a holiday to visit Montserrat in the Catalonian region of Spain. The peaks of Montserrat stand over 1100 metres above sea level. There is a famous abbey housing the legendary Black Madonna. And then there is a cable car which ascends to the tip of the mountain, where you can visit various abandoned hovels in the cliff faces which were the former abodes of reclusive monks.

Having made the decision to go on holiday to Spain and purchased the trip, the man began worrying about the upcoming holiday. How would he cope? What terrors the thought of being that high up a mountain caused him. This poor man's heightened state of anxiety lasted many weeks until finally the day of the holiday arrived.

The journey to Spain went well, the accommodation in Barcelona was superb. In retrospect the man realised from that point, he was no longer worrying about going on the holiday. In fact he could actually say he was enjoying the holiday, if only he could stop worrying about the day of the trip to Montserrat.

Inevitably that day came and he boarded the coach that would take the road up the mountain to the abbey. He was now no longer worried about the day coming, it was here, he was doing it. Now he was worried about arriving at the top of the mountain.

The coach eventually ended its ascent having gone as far as it could go. The rest of the ascent would be done by cable car. At this point however, the man's anxiety got the better of him. He told his wife and son that he really could go no further, this was his limit; he had come as far as he was able. He had suffered weeks of anxiety over this trip. He urged them to go and experience without him, which they did, grateful to him for making the effort thus far.

The coach had stopped in a car park, which could have been a car park anywhere. It was built in the centre of a largish flat area, a plateau. The man brought his attention onto how he was actually feeling considering he was over 1000 metres above sea level. He realised as the ground around him was flat, he didn't feel high up and hence he began to relax a little, glad all this worry was finally over.

He reflected on those months of worry and anxiety culminating at this point. He realised that right here, right now is quite pleasant, and he began to explore a little to pass the time. The area was interesting, peculiar rocks and interesting flora grabbing the man's attention. Then suddenly he became aware that his wanderings had taken him to the very edge of a sheer drop. Fear gripped him again. But as he stood on the edge of the cliff, he realised he was wasn't worried about being on the edge anymore, rather his actual concern now was about falling off. And in that moment also he further realised, if he did fall off, he would no longer be worried about falling off, but rather he would be worried about landing!

It was in that moment he understood - worry was always about a future event, never about what is actually happening now!

One of the options he had in the moment was simply to step back and return the way he came, which he did.

The months of worry and anxiety had been suffering for no reason. Worrying about the holiday, then worrying about the day, and then worrying about reaching the top. The worry was always a mental projection of what was to come. He was never worried about this moment now. He has since learned to enjoy the now, to live each moment and not worry about it until or unless it comes, which in essence means no worry as in actuality we get on with now, not worry about it.

Living in the Moment disables worry by enabling us to place our attention on what is happening now, and make relevant decisions and choices from the options we have right now.

That thing you so desire – is it here now? You may move towards it, but do not be so focused on the future that you miss what is happening in each moment along the way.

That worry you have, that fear of something happening – is it happening now? If not deal with it when that moment comes, if ever it does. Remember worry exists only in your projection of the future – always. Worry is merely a thought. You never worry **about** now. You just worry now about something that is not here. Choose to live with now as it mostly is quite pleasant. Yes of course not nice things happen. When they do however, we deal with them. Those moments provide different options, different choices, and ones we never dreamed of when we were previously worrying.

Everything is transitory. Nothing lasts exactly as it is. That is the nature of life. Everything changes moment by moment. What does this actual moment feel like? What are you actually aware of now? Do you live your life missing now, because you are always projecting your thoughts forward or backwards, therefore either re-experiencing what has happened already or scared of what you presume may come?

Acceptance

Accept this moment as it is. There is no need to grab hold of it, nor any need to dismiss it or reject it. In actuality you can't. What is, is. In this moment you cannot change it. It is as it is, acceptance is simply realising that.

Acceptance is not giving in. It is accepting that right here, right now in this particular moment this is the way it is; this is the point from which I will move. Know that moment, know that situation, not your projections of it, not your desires of it, not dismissing the bits you don't want of it, but exploring what it is and knowing it as it really is, devoid of all the fantasy your mind is adding to it.

Accept that as each moment passes it changes. You can choose to move away from it, or you may choose to stay with it, but first you have to 'see' what it is and also you have to acknowledge and accept that in the next moment, something will be different anyway.   You do not need to pretend anything about it nor is there any benefit in doing so.

Only from point of acceptance do you ever have any real choice.   If you are resisting something, you are affecting your interaction with it.   You can say 'I don't like this' or 'I do like this', but you can only say either when you have accepted what it is.   Until you accept, you don't move, you keep yourself immobile.

An instance of this occurred with this very piece of work. Following a solid six hour session working on my laptop, I lost the manuscript – it didn't save. I spent my free hours of that and the next day thinking of every way I may be able to retrieve it. I spent the day after that very stressed because I couldn't. I didn't work at all. I was stuck, resisting the fact I had lost all that work.

Then I remembered it was about Mindfulness. In applying Mindfulness, I accepted that what I had done in print was gone.   Until that acceptance occurred I was literally stuck, unable to move forward from that point of loss, feeling unable and being unwilling to carry on and redo it. I realised I had mentally held onto that moment and made it my own experienced existence for three days. That moment didn't stay, it moved on in reality. In reality many other things happened in those three days, yet I experienced that moment because I held my attention on it and refused to accept it was, but now it has gone.

Having accepted it was gone, it lost intensity. Suddenly it was not such a tragedy. I didn't feel the need to be upset and angry anymore, so I wasn't. Accepting it was gone and there was nothing I could do about it because that is the way it is, I began again with peace of mind. The fact is, it was not such a tragic event that I need have wasted three days stressing about it. I didn't enjoy anything else in those days. My attention was focused on my own belief that it was not right, not fair. I felt all the emotions involved with those thoughts, all negative ones of course. Despite that self-imposed suffering, the fact remained it had gone. It just had.

I now see it is my choice at what point I accept. Therefore it is my choice how long I proverbially bang my own head against a brick wall and endure the consequences of that self-inflicted suffering.

I also accept it was very frustrating and extremely annoying. But I could have accepted that frustration and annoyance in the moment it happened, given them their moments, and then moved on. But I resisted. For three days I refused to simply accept the facts.

As we experience using Mindfulness we will become very aware of things about ourselves; how we have habitual ways of thinking and reacting particularly. We may realise we have thoughts and feelings we don't cognitively agree with. Accept these things. Don't try to hide them from yourself as if they don't exist. Don't try and make them something other than what they are, merely accept. Only from point of acceptance can you change if you want to, or move forward or around if you want to. Only by accepting it is there, here and now, can you effectively move on.

Often we do not accept how we think or feel because we believe we shouldn't think or feel that way. We judge what is and resist. We feed our self-illusion, we turn away from the truth and as a consequence we remain stuck in that very situation. Whether we should or shouldn't feel that way is irrelevant. There is no should or shouldn't at this point, there only is what is. Only from the point of accepting it exists can we change it for the next moments if we want to.

Acceptance isn't only about the negative stuff. If you feel good, feel good now. Allow that. So many situations exist in the same moments. Do you deprive yourself of the good ones because you place your attention on the bad ones? We do actually think ourselves out of feeling good because we resist so much, – accept what feels good with each moment, awaken to that and accept that is also in this moment, because most of it we miss.

If you feel pain, don't fight it, don't resist it or try to pretend it isn't there; accept you feel pain and know it is for a reason. Acknowledge it without judgement. From that point, you have a choice to move from it, or ease it, but first you have to accept it hurts. Pain is a warning, don't mask it without first acknowledging it has something to tell you. There is a reason for it. The process of trying to resist, lengthens and strengthens the unpleasantness you feel.

There are times when life hurts, physically, emotionally or mentally. Pain, discomfort and not having what we want, when and the way we want it, is part of life. None of us can avoid that. Accept it and then choose from available options for the next moment.

Acceptance in these terms also require we acknowledge our expectations. In the practice of Mindfulness, the point is to release expectations and accept things as they are, not how we think they should be or how we want them to be.

Non-Judgement

Observe everything as if you are an onlooker, a reporter or researcher maybe. Get to know it, don't presume to know it. Carry out an unbiased, unprejudiced inquiry. To inquire is to explore. It is to question without pre-knowledge.

Do not view everything in terms of right or wrong, good or bad – see them simply as being. If something does not feel good, or it is not helpful, this can and will change moment by moment. In this instant the task is to become aware about it, do not judge it - see it, feel it, get to know it for yourself. Pre-judge or presume nothing.

In a course I had the privilege of co-hosting, my partner illustrated this principle further. She invited the participants to choose something to eat from the array of foods she had provided. However she told them not to eat it. Instead she asked them to listen to it. Of course they were bemused by this. Hear it? What she was illustrating was how we presume and prejudge everything. Who says it doesn't have a sound? Maybe it doesn't but do we ever bother to know that for our self? Do we ever prove our own perceived truths to ourselves? Gunaratana states, don't simply believe because some wise man said. Know your own truth (1).

Seeing Anew

This is akin to seeing anew. Do not presume you already know about anything, find out now in this moment. You will always find out that you don't really know at all. So many things you have seen before, but have you? Question it, pay attention in this moment as if you are seeing for the first time.

What about everything you never noticed before? You will see something new every time. You can see everything and know it again in each moment because in reality, in each different moment, it is different.

As humans we tend to live in a very predetermined way. Our past experience tends to dictate the manner in which we approach anything we think/feel we have come across before. We think we know it already so we pay it no attention, and react to it in our usual habitual way.

What about our family or friends? Do you know them? Maybe that sounds strange, but do you know them now in this moment, or are you simply accepting as reality they are as you have predetermined they are?

The mental discipline of Mindfulness helps you to stop doing that. This in turn changes your experience, of everything and that tends to change the course of life as you break out of your own predetermined rut.

Seeing-Anew also helps you see things from other people's point of view. When someone is saying something you don't agree with, rather than dictate your truth, look at the subject again. Mentally inquire as to how they may be viewing it that way. It may be you continue to disagree. That's ok. What will have happened despite that is you will know something more.

Seeing anew helps us with our own egos. It is our culture to be judged on our ability to relay facts as we have been taught them. Our whole education system is built on that premise. We don't like being told or even thinking we are misinformed. Why is this? Why hamper our initial exploratory stance in life, that stance we had as a child when everything was new and exciting. They say that as a child our brains are like a sponge, they simple sup it all up, take it all in. What changed? Maybe nothing but physical, maybe it was us deciding we already know and simply not seeing anymore.

I can personally vouch for the fact that when you take this attitude of seeing anew, the world, indeed life, takes on a new and exciting perspective. If you can achieve stopping yourself from thinking 'I already know that' and look or hear again, you really do find out something more. You may confirm what you have seen or heard before, that's ok. Some attendees of the aforementioned course, did not hear their food. That's ok, some did! If you take an open exploratory stance to absolutely everything, I guarantee life takes on a depth and richness that was not there before.

Do not take for granted because someone else said, see for yourself.

Experience everything as if you are experiencing for the first time.

Above all, enjoy the good stuff and then really enjoy again and again.

Non-Striving

In every first time relaxation session I have held, there is always at least one person who says "I can't do it, I can't relax". That is because they are striving or trying to relax.

The act of trying automatically invokes a resistance. The art is to allow, not try. Allowing lets something come to you or happen. It is passive. To try is to strive.

It is our culture to try, and to try hard. We are taught from a young age that to try hard is good, it will get us everything we want and that not trying hard enough is nearly always the named reason for perceived failure. We paddle against the tide and make life so hard. We have totally forgotten that actually we could just sit in our boat, go with the flow and enjoy what life brings as we float along (18).

Of course some things require effort, but we forget that most 'moments' don't require effort. Self-discipline is required and beneficial, but self-discipline is different from striving. It will require self-discipline to put aside moments to practice Mindfulness. However you can never strive to do Mindfulness; you take in the principles, you experience your meditation, the rest you allow. When you allow, when the expectation and the striving goes, it happens all by itself.

Life in moments unfolds before us, and it does whether we are trying or not. Don't strive for the moment, allow it to be.

You cannot try to meditate or to relax. That is an opposition of terms. You allow yourself to meditate or relax. You do place your attention on purpose to some aspect of your existence, we commonly in insight mediation for example place our attention on breathing. However, if there is a sudden noise, simply accept there is a noise. It will have grabbed your attention. That is ok. Our attention is supposed to be grabbed by a loud noise, it could denote danger. You acknowledge it, you acknowledge your own reaction to it, you become aware it became part of your meditation experience and then you place your attention to rest back on what you were meditating on. By doing this, you allow; then the relaxation occurs all by itself.

When you feel a stress or tension, don't try to release it, acknowledge it, become aware of it without judgement and without resistance, acknowledge what is also in this moment, bring your focus of attention back to your breathing and then that tension releases itself. What you have to do is allow; stop striving. Allowing occurs with acceptance.

All of these principles interplay with each other. Allow them to go into your awareness as a flow; intermingling and interacting with each other as they will all by themselves. They are principles and as you live by them, they will take on various applications. As you allow these principles into your life, they become applicable to everything.

This won't happen day 1, because it is a progress, a journey. It builds by itself when you allow.

Remember we said before, Mindfulness is never finished. It will always be work-in-progress. It will always continue to improve and in turn it will continue to improve your experience of life.

The Purposeful Placing of Attention

A cornerstone of Mindfulness Practice is realising that our experience of each moment depends on how and where our attention is placed. How and what we direct our awareness to in each moment, dictates what experience we will have of that moment.

Let's look at the what. There are millions of things happening in this moment. Your awareness, your attention could be on any one of them. Odds are that at any random moment, your attention is not on this moment at all; rather it may be ruminating about what a colleague said to you yesterday, particularly if it upset you. Or you may be worrying about what you have to do one day next week. In either of these cases, your experience of this moment won't be of the realities of this moment. Rather, in the case of the former, you will be re-experiencing yesterday. In the case of the latter, you will be experiencing your own future forecast, your own imagination's prediction of next week. Neither is reality and potentially never will be.

Those thoughts, that thing on which you place your attention, will bring about feelings in you; they will bring about an emotional response. If the thing you have to do next week is a negative thing, your emotional response will be negative emotions – fear, concern, distress, anxiety or sadness. In that moment you will be feeling those emotions; you will be suffering. It does not matter that event or circumstance is not happening now, the fact that your attention is placed there, you will experience it. Whatever your thought is, even if it is not happening now, even though it is not reality now, nor may it ever be so, you will be experiencing the emotions relevant to that thought now just as if it existed now.

Conversely, if the situation that is happening next week is a lovely one, then those thoughts will produce nice emotions, excitement, happiness, wonder. However that event is still not happening now, even though you are experiencing those emotions. Hence we talk about positive thinking. How often have we been encouraged to think positively, or encouraged someone else to do so. Sometimes that is so hard. It is easier and more stable to bring our attention to now, this moment, the real one. We can consciously and on purpose place our attention on one of the many myriads of things that is happening in this moment now. There are positive things about this moment now.

So we begin to realise that our own experience of life in this moment has not been necessarily of actual life in this moment. We have been experiencing the subject of our thoughts, namely those things on which we have placed our attention.

Let's combine the 'how' with the 'what' we are placing our attention on. Whilst writing the last paragraph, a fly entered the room and was, in my perception, buzzing around noisily. It grabbed my attention, and as it did so, my experience of the fly magnified. It felt like it was buzzing around my head; it felt, (sounded?) very loud. I associate flies with maggots and disease, hence I began ensuring it did not go anywhere near my cup of tea. Soon my complete attention was engrossed on this fly and stopping it from causing worldwide contamination. My mind had added so much to the actual event! My emotional response was agitation, annoyance, disgust. I even experienced anger as I was feeling like I couldn't continue writing, that it was killing my concentration, putting me off doing what I needed to be doing. Yes me, I accept how out of proportion this minor situation had become. Luckily I practice Mindfulness regularly, and it has become second nature to me now to identify more than one thing in each moment, and choose where I place my attention. Yes second nature I said. Even though I practice Mindfulness very regularly, I am still on a journey.

However, on purpose, it took less than a second to look out the window and notice it was a bright sunny day again today. I glanced across the room and saw my black Labrador laying on the sofa with his head placed perfectly on my cushion; he looked so sweet it made me smile. As I smiled at my dog, the emotion I felt was tenderness, love and enjoyment. This banished the anger and annoyance I had felt. And then, on purpose, I brought my own attention back to my laptop and this writing, and I read the last two lines and began again. The fly continues flying. As I think of it, as I place my attention on it, I am more aware of it, and it sounds louder. It is not good, it is not bad; it simply is, along with all the other things that are existing in this moment also. It does not stop me writing, nor will it contaminate my world. Those conclusions were simply my thoughts, it was not reality.

In the moment I saw my dog, I became unaware of the fly. Because it didn't have my attention, it was not a part of my experienced existence. I chose what to place my attention on, I chose what would occupy my thoughts and I literally changed my experience of that moment. Both things were there in reality, both the fly and my dog, but whichever had my attention I would experience or feel, accordingly.

These are some of the most beautiful and fundamental practices of Mindfulness. Becoming aware, on purpose, of this moment. Living in the moment and choosing how to live this moment; acknowledging the ability we all have to change perspective and in doing so change our own experience of life in this moment. This literally is a life-changing practice.

Another way to change how we experience this moment is by acknowledging and then choosing 'how' we are perceiving it. Sometimes things do occupy our attention, they do need to and they may not be pleasant. However, HOW you perceive it, in what manner you perceive it, will likewise change your experience of it.

For example, once you have accepted what is and get on with it, does it feel a bit smaller? Often our resistance to accepting things feeds them, makes them larger or bigger or more terrifying. At least ninety per cent of the time, things we have been worrying about are not half so bad when we get there as our minds had made them out to be. If we stop and examine this moment in which this 'thing' whatever it may be, exists, is it really so awful or is it unpleasant? Has it really ruined our life, or has it ruined a plan? Has it really destroyed you or has it made you really sad? Did the fly really stop me from writing?

How you are thinking will cause how you are feeling. Are you suffering more than you actually need to because of the words you are using to yourself?

Words have phenomenal power. Words cause feelings. Try it now. If I say 'We have a problem?' How does that make you feel?

Now if I say 'We have a challenge?' How does that feel? There is a difference.

If you are telling yourself something has ruined your life, you will be experiencing emotions pertaining to something having ruined life. That is unpleasant. That is suffering. If you though acknowledge that it is extremely annoying rather than having ruined your life, your emotions will follow accordingly. Those feelings are much less unpleasant, you are now irritated rather than destroyed.

The next moment you are feeling bad, pay attention to it, all of it, get to know what bad really is. Question whether your level of suffering is greater than it need be. Explore what bad really is. I say this because I think in most cases you will find it is not so bad. Bold statement that may be, but true nevertheless.

This is why Mindfulness Practice is now commonly used in Pain Clinics. Learning not to mentally exaggerate what is, brings the emotion and the physiology in line with what is. Learning to stop the resistance to it and accepting actually reduces pain, even further. Learning to place your attention on purpose to an area of choice, literally learning to take your mind of it, massively lowers your experience of the pain. It has verifiable, proven results.

I worked with one patient who suffered continuous pain in his head. This pain interfered with his sleep, his work and his relationships. However when he played table tennis the 'pain went'. Did it? Yes, because he became unaware of the pain, literally unaware. Therefore when he was playing table tennis the pain did not exist. He played table tennis very well. He was rarely beaten. This is not surprising, because his mind, his attention was so consumed by the processes involved in playing, it did not register the pain. Because he was unaware of the pain, in his experienced life in those moments, his pain did not exist. I was tempted to say at this point that his playing table-tennis, did not physiologically alter whatever was hurting in his head, but actually that is not so. It is also becoming proven fact that physiology does react significantly to both thought and emotion (17). Hence

Mindfulness is finding increasing application in many specific fields of physical healthcare.

Thought and emotion have impact on the nervous system obviously, but also massive impact on the immune system, and digestive system. Stress and emotional response is thought to be the trigger for the onset of many different diseases and disorders. Whilst many of us carry the genes for particular conditions, stress and/or trauma are the most common activator. Suffering is dis-ease. Our own healthcare system, the NHS, recognises there is 'No Health without Mental Health' (3).

Put simply, we experience what our attention is on. There is no point mentally clinging onto the good things, avoiding the bad things and paying very little attention to anything in the middle. The fact is we cannot grab hold of the good things, we can only enjoy them to their utmost extent when they are in this moment by placing our full attention on them. Neither can we avoid bad things, sometimes they exist whether we want them to or not. How much attention we give to them is our choice. They happen despite our best attempts and plans. Acknowledge they exist along with all the other things that exist in this moment. Everything exists for moments, but then it is gone, including the bad stuff.

The only predetermined human journey is to experience. We inevitably experience joy and suffering. They provide contrast (18). We choose however, how much of our attention we wish to give either. We have the ability to realise all the other things that are existing in every moment simultaneously. By choice we can place our attention. So many things are in each moment that we never see, purely because we don't pay attention and see; we are not aware of them.

Mindfulness runs into reality. It takes it full on, here and now. Mindfulness is not escapism, it is not dreamland. It gets you to realise what actually is. It gets you to become an observer of now, to witness and feel and register the actual experience of now. You can see everything and anything for what it really is, without prejudice, without striving, and with the knowledge that in the next moment it is gone; nothing remains the same. You begin to see everything in life as transitory and you begin to be able to pick what and how you want to experience to a much greater degree.

Meditation

Meditation has come to mean many different things to different people. There are different ways to meditate.

Mindfulness uses Vipassana meditation. This is often translated as Insight Meditation, since the purpose of it is to give the meditator insight into the nature of reality and understanding of their own existence. In the words of Gunaratana, its intention is to pick apart the screen of lies and delusions through which we normally view the world, thus to reveal the face of ultimate reality (1).

Meditation is not JUST a relaxation technique, however relaxation is a key component of meditation. All meditation procedures bring the mind to rest on one specific. When you return your attention to your breathing, as breathing is initially what you will be meditating on, think of your attention as coming back to rest.

Meditate enough, and you achieve a deep relaxation. Once achieved, this relaxed state can be called upon whenever you need it. As discussed earlier if you use a cue or an anchor in NLP terms, you can literally trigger a relaxed state at will, or on cue, just as we accept we can trigger an anxious state (23).

Meditation allows time out from external bombardments of stress, pressures and worries.

Meditation is not a quick cure-all. You will start seeing changes right away, but really profound effects come in time. From each session you gain results, but the immediate results are often very subtle. However, other results are occurring deep within the mind, and they do manifest later. These results are life changing.

"One day you've got a problem that looks absolutely unsolvable, an enormous muddle of maybes, uncertainties and barriers. The next day you are thinking about nothing particularly when the solution just pops out of the deep mind. You say, 'Ah ha!' and the whole thing is solved. This intuitive solution only occurs when you disengage your logic circuits from the problem and give the deep mind the opportunity to create a solution from the vast library of knowledge we all have". *Gunaratana* (1).

Meditation allows you to disentangle yourself from your preconditioned cognitive thought processes. It is the art of stepping out of your own way mentally. It is a practical skill that focuses on everyday events and has immediate application in everybody's life.

Patience is the key and through meditation, you will learn patience. However, it is a happy patience, not a frustrated one.

When you are facilitating a Mindfulness Meditation session, be it by yourself, in a group or in a one to one situation, remember and where applicable, communicate the following:

If you feel yourself becoming involved or caught up in your own thoughts or feelings, return your attention to your breathing. Do this on purpose. Direct your attention back to rest on how you breathe and how that feels.

Don't cling to anything; don't reject anything: Allow everything to flow, unfold. Let come what comes and merely observe it, whatever it is.

If nice mental images arise, that is fine. If unpleasant mental images arise, that is fine, too. Look on all of it as equal and allow yourself to be comfortable with whatever arises. Don't fight against thoughts popping into your attention, just observe it all mindfully and then rest back on your breathing.

If an outside distraction takes your attention, don't fight it, allow it. Note that was your experience. Note the noise or whatever it was took your attention, acknowledge that with acceptance. It is ok. Then place your attention back to rest on your breathing.

You cannot do meditation wrong. Whatever experience you had, you had. It is the art of being aware of that experience you are cultivating. The only job you have to do is to replace your attention back on your breathing each time you have acknowledged something else. As you practice this will automatically become easier and easier and you will find you notice less and less distractions. This happens all by itself, it is a process.

The Practice

As we stated earlier, many therapists or practitioners require you meditate for 45 minutes each day and commit to this. Jon Kabat-Zinn's clinic required patients and practitioners to do the meditative exercise for 45 minutes daily. The therapeutic benefit is in meditating for a period of time, regularly. You do have to acknowledge a commitment to yourself. You do have to have the intention of giving yourself every chance. This does require a commitment to yourself, a self-discipline.

However, I have also stated that due to working with acutely ill patients, dictating the 45 minute criteria as a prerequisite would have meant Mindfulness was not available to all. When acutely ill some had trouble keeping their attention on one thing for 60 seconds, let alone 45 minutes. I continue to debate my case on this point.

I have facilitated a Mindfulness session with a patient who was in a manic state. It was different. It was a lot more animated than I was used to, but he was doing it with me. It was a new and endearing experience and it progressed from that point. I do accept it was continuously guided, but so be it – that's ok. When his mania subsided, he took the experience with him and practiced alone. I heard Mindfulness Meditation has become a relapse prevention strategy for him.

Therein lies the importance I feel. We all have to start somewhere. The benefits start at the beginning, wherever that beginning may be. It is in the spirit of Mindfulness to say we are at where we are at. We are at the point, state, situation, whatever, that we are. That is ok and Mindfulness accepts whatever is in this moment to be applicable here and now.

When facilitating groups or one to one sessions on the acute ward, we started slowly, and we would guide them. They would follow for a time, then wander. Being with them, I was able to gently assist them to bring their awareness back to their breathing again and again, sometimes beginning with only ten minutes, sometimes some were able to keep with half hour of guided meditation straight away. It was individual, personal. But from whatever start point, the building was a gradual process and it was always beneficial.

I always asked the participants to do it by themselves at least once a day, more if they could and be aware of the building up of the length of time they did. Some did, some didn't, and the range of benefits spoke for themselves. However even those that didn't, benefitted from what they did do.

This is not a get out clause. As Kabat-Zin states, self-discipline and intentionality are paramount (2). There is a discipline to Mindfulness. Self-discipline is a commitment to yourself. Self-discipline in this case is saying I am important enough to have this time for myself, to keep myself well, or to enable my recovery. I acknowledge my body needs food and water and I know that in order to maintain my wellbeing, I have to apply the self-discipline to eat. It is the same for Mindfulness practice. But build up is still a discipline. Striving is not required. It is my experience that it is ok to start gently.

When you are ready to practice Mindfulness as a discipline, do ensure you set aside 45 minutes each day. Do prepare for this time, making it an important time. Do treat this time with the utmost respect. What it is ultimately doing for you is immeasurable in terms of benefits. Beneficial things should be cherished. You should be cherished. This is a pleasant, peaceful and truly wonderful journey to be embarking on. You will know that for yourself very soon.

You will feel peaceful for so much more of the day; you will sleep better at night. You will experience so much more happiness and you will be able to meet life's challenges and make informed choices from so many available options.

Life doesn't become full of roses all of a sudden; life remains as it is. It is you who change; it is you who begins to live so many more moments and gain so much more from your own existence.

So let's get to it. Please read the section below as many times as it takes for you to get a good understanding of what you will be doing.

Then do it.

Remember you can't get it wrong, there is no right or wrong. Yes it will improve with practice, what doesn't. Enjoy the experience and enjoy the benefits.

Don't try hard: Don't force anything or make any exaggerated efforts. Meditation is not aggressive. There is no striving. Allow any effort be relaxed and steady.

Don't rush: There is no hurry, so take you time. Settle yourself and sit as though you have a whole day. Anything really valuable takes time to develop.

Initially, whilst you are learning sit in a position that is comfortable but upright. Loosen any tight clothing, belts or laces. Do not fold your arms or cross your legs. Sit in an open position allowing your circulation to work at its uttermost, do not impede your own circulation. If you can or if you want to at a later date, adopt a yogic posture. The importance of yoga is the form, the holding the body in a beneficial stance in tune with your breathing.

As you meditate, you will have thoughts, you will have feelings, you will have physiological responses. Have no expectation of what should or shouldn't occur. Just allow what occurs to occur and observe it. Then rest your attention back on your breath.

One of the mental disciplines you are learning is to observe in the detached manner of an observer without judgement or prejudice; without holding onto or resisting, without getting emotionally involved. Observing is passive. You do not need to become involved with what you are observing over and above gaining an understanding of it. You are simply observing your own experience. You are becoming aware.

You can experience and observe at the same time. This is 'awareness'. This is the blending of thought and feeling, blending of the heart and mind, full awareness.

Begin by observing your breathing. I recommend initially take two slightly deeper than normal breaths just to give yourself something stated to begin placing your attention on. Following the two deeper breaths allow your breathing to return to normal and do what it wants to do. Watch it, see it and observe what it does.

Whilst breathing we are interacting, exchanging gases with our environment and those around us. We are producing changes in our environment and our environment is causing changes in us. We can observe this.

We can feel how it feels when we breathe, we can feel how our bodies react, how they move, where we can feel the breath. We can experience the sense of calm awareness our breathing brings. We can observe our own reaction to that. We can feel changes in temperature, in our nose if we breathe in cold air, how it warms as it comes out through our mouth maybe.

Do not worry about whether you can do it, or if there's too much noise or something is putting you off.

If something distracts your attention away from your breathing, know you are experiencing that moment, pay attention to it. When you notice the noise or the something, detach yourself, become the observer and observe your own reactions to it.

The point of Visapanna meditation is to become aware, non-judgementally, of your own reactions to things, of your own experience of things.

When you hear the noise, you may feel angry, disappointed or let down. You may startle, or you may tense-up. You may find the noise propels your thoughts onto something else. Habitual thoughts? Observe this process in yourself. Where does it start – what is the first thought/feeling? What is the next one? Where does it go? What does it feel like? What emotion did you experience? What happened physiologically – did you tense-up, did your heart begin to beat faster? What words, what head chatter automatically came to mind? These are the things you are observing. Become aware of your own experience – this is the point. Once you have observed and got to know your reaction to the distraction, then, on purpose, place your attention back onto your breathing and allow it to rest there.

As the observer of yourself, resist the temptation to mentally narrate, to put into words, to judge or to mentally typecast or formulate.

As the observer, you cannot grab hold of any experience, you cannot keep it; you are merely observing the flow, much like watching a film at the cinema. If you begin a mental narration of what just happened you will miss the next bit.

Likewise you cannot reject any unpleasantness. As the observer, just be – just observe, just let it play out. Allow and see. This is Vipassana meditation. This is the discipline you are learning – you are learning to become aware of yourself as an interconnected part of your environment.

You will be able to see, observe and become aware of: physiological feelings, pressure, touch, changes of heart and breathing rates; emotional feelings, and how they actually feel; thoughts in the form of words or pictures; and you will also observe your automatic reactions to these. You will become aware of your own habitual way of reacting to things around or within you.

Be gentle with yourself: Be kind to yourself. You are. There are many wonderful things about you, there are many unhelpful ways you react, but even these are done with good intentions so get to know them. Know and acknowledge all of you without judgement. The process of becoming who you will be begins first with the total acceptance of who you are now in this very moment. The point is to observe yourself, your own thoughts, feelings and reactions. You are calmly without judgement, without expectation, just getting to know what you do, feel and think. You, most likely for the first time, are really getting to know you. And when you do it again tomorrow, you will see you are different. That happened all by itself.

Don't fight with what you experience, just observe it all mindfully.

Following your meditation, you do not need to analyse this experience. This form of seeing, becoming aware, is to experience. When it is finished, you have had it, it is done. It is gone as with every experience we have. However the memory of it is left in your subconscious and it will begin working for you. Remember 'of the memory', the original Sanskrit meaning of Mindfulness. Don't tamper with this memory by analysing, just let it be as it is.

What you will begin to notice in time is that you have more knowledge, more understanding about yourself. You have a new knowledge and understanding about yourself and you have created another perspective in which to experience any experience. You became aware of how you react, you became aware of how you felt and to what and where that went. It is this that will influence future experiences. You have given yourself another perspective and another choice and you will continue to do so. In this sense, existence is limitless. There are so many possibilities, so many variations and combinations. Nothing is ever, ever the same again.

By default, deeper understanding of yourself gives you deeper understanding of others. You do not have to try for this – it simply happens. When you have the wisdom to truly understand a situation, compassion towards all parties occurs by default.

You become aware as you realise each second of every day is a new experience in its own right.

How you react to each experience eventually becomes a matter of choice, made in each moment; nothing taken for granted, nothing pre-emptied, nothing prejudged.

Everything is seen anew, which is as it really is. Yesterday was not the same as today, tomorrow will be very different.

We realise reality does not exist in the past or in the future. The past and the future are merely mental projections. There is only reality now – this very moment, and that reality is fluid, it flows and it changes, moment by moment.

You truly begin to awaken, to live each moment and appreciate that life's richness of experience is always here, now.

Enjoy.

Walking Meditation

Walking Vipassana meditation is done the same way as above, but your eyes are open, you are moving and your attention is placed on the process of walking rather than the process of breathing.

Like breathing, walking has many aspects to it and you are exploring this. What muscles move, which part of the foot touches the floor first, which part lifts first? What is the sensation when the foot is in the air, what is it when the foot is on the ground?

There is so much to explore, to become truly aware of walking, and trust me, you never will. You will never know all the sensations as your nervous system carries messages to and from your brain, but you will develop an awareness of that process.

Likewise, as with the breathing meditation, you will experience distractions. That's ok, acknowledge them, know them and then simply place your attention to rest on your walking again.

It is different to walk on grass with bare feet. It is different to walk on a rug with bare feet. It is different to walk in shoes. And it is simply different each time anyway, so remember, however many times you do this, you have never done this one before. See anew each time.

Three Minute Meditation

This meditation is used a lot when sharing Mindfulness in the Workplace. In the same manner as above, meditate on, or become aware of yourself in your immediate environment, the office chair, the queue in the canteen, the frozen section of the supermarket. Just take some moments, three minutes of them to know yourself in this environment. To check in with yourself. It's like saying to yourself, 'Hi – how are you doing?' Obviously in this meditation exercise you are not bringing your mind back to rest at any point, you are doing a three minute check over.

It's really helpful to do this before you start a period of work, check into what mood you are in, how you are feeling physically and where your head is at. Or how does this chair feel? Or am I seated appropriately before I begin a large volume of work. It can be whatever, so long as it is developing an awareness of you right here, right now. Also before you take a break. Check your own stress levels, let the break be a break not a continuation of that mental chattering.

You will be surprised what taking notice of yourself brings. I felt the urge to type a little smiley then as sometimes it is quite amusing.

Do you know how you habitually sit? Do you know what you habitually do in the queue? Have you ever paid yourself some attention?

Mindful Reflection

It is advised that you do not analyse your meditation following it. You have your meditation session, it finishes, it has ended, leave it alone. The benefits from doing it will happen all by themselves, both in physical and mental terms. The reason we are advised not to analyse following meditation is your conscious, which includes everything that makes up your ego, and all the connections that lead you from one thought automatically to the next AND all the schemas and filters you have devised over the years, will change the experience. What we are trying to achieve with meditation is that free-flow from subconscious to conscious which will happen all by itself and which will all by itself affect the ego if we allow it and not use the ego, the schemas and filters and the automatic connections to judge or analyse it.

The other reason is, if you begin a meditation with a view to recounting it after, either mentally or verbally, you are very likely to induce a mental running narrative throughout the meditation. One of the purposes of meditation is to stop this process, for the period of the meditation. We already know how hard this is, our conscious mind continuously butts into our meditation and we persevere in bringing our attention back to the focus of the meditation. So obviously we do not want to start the meditation with the intention of building a mental narrative about it.

Sometimes however it is good to reflect, not on your meditation necessarily, but on various things.

Reflecting is obviously looking back, and it should be noticed there is a big difference between reflection and rumination. Rumination is your mind taking control again and it keeps going back to the same thoughts over and over. Not only is this tiring but it is also cementing your automatic thought patterns as each time that neural network is used it strengthens.

Mindful reflection is reflecting back on an event or thought or emotion whilst applying the principles of Mindfulness. So you are reflecting with the intention of getting to know the event, thought or emotion, without judgement and with acceptance. You are developing an awareness about that upon which you are reflecting.

Again start with that intention. Sit comfortably and assist your circulation and breathing to do their thing by loosening tight clothing, sitting upright. Take the two slightly deeper than normal breaths to start as this cues your Mindful stance. It becomes almost like a meditation but the subject of your meditation is you giving conscious thought to the subject of your reflection. When I do this, it is like experiencing a meditation occurring in the background and your reflection occurring in the foreground. It is like rerunning a film taken of you living the event, or feeling the feeling and the Vipassana meditation gives you a deep insight into how you are reacting to it now.

That is my experience of it, but however it works or feels for you is ok remember. Your intention is to see, become aware of a truth. The purpose of Mindful Reflection is to develop an unaltered awareness of what occurred. It is very enlightening and helpful in understanding yourself.

A Relaxation Technique

It is good to begin meditation with relaxation and if you meditate soundly enough, you will achieve a deep relaxation.

Once achieved, this relaxed state can be called upon whenever and wherever you need it.

Concentration and relaxation are considered necessary concomitants to awareness. The purpose of Mindful meditation is to develop awareness. Increased awareness is a safeguard against danger. Increased awareness negates both the need for and thus the presence of stress and anxiety. So I always advise to begin each meditation with relaxation.

Relaxation techniques are also a useful introduction to meditation. The following can be practised by yourself or in a group. It's called a body scan and is a great way to ease tensions held in your body.

If you are doing it by yourself, read through a couple of times to get the general gist. Again, don't be concerned about doing it wrong. If you miss a bit out, it doesn't matter, just make a mental note and it is unlikely you will miss it out next time.

Likewise, if you are facilitating a group, read through it a few times before you begin, so you have a good idea of where you are going. Then you can either recite from memory, or you can read from a script. Remember to pause though! Let the participants have time to not only carry out your instruction, but enough time also to savour the moment.

Let's take a few minutes to relax your body and mind right now. Ensure you are sitting comfortably and not impeding your circulation in any way; this could be uncrossing your legs or loosening any tight clothing.

We'll begin with a few slow, deep breaths. Each time you breathe in, breathe all the way down into your stomach. Breathe in slowly through your nose, and feel your abdomen and lungs expand with air. Don't rush to breathe in.

After drawing in a long deep breath, allow your breath to flow back out through your mouth. Just let go of each breath, and with it, release any tension or stress you might have been holding on to. You might like to mentally repeat the word "relax" as you breathe out.

Try this now; slowly draw in a deep breath through your nose. Just gradually fill your lungs and abdomen with air, and when they are full, release that breath completely; let your jaw go and allow that air out through your mouth.

You are beginning to feel yourself relaxing. Your breath will dissolve tension just as easily as warm water melts ice.

Breathe in once again. Feel your body fill with air ...and when you are ready, release the breath, let it flow out naturally. Breathe all the way out until your lungs are empty.

Let's draw in a third and final breath, nice and deep. Feel yourself relaxing as you gradually release the breath.

Now let your breathing return to a normal rhythm. Don't rush, take as long as you like.

Become aware of your resting breathing pattern as we begin to scan over your body, looking for areas of tension to release. Let your breath take the rhythm it wants.

As I mention each body part, bring your awareness to it, tense it for a moment and then let it relax. Notice the feeling of relaxation as you do this with each area of your body. Notice how nice it feels as you let go.

It is quite common for people to store a lot of tension in their jaw muscles, so let's begin there. Pay attention to your jaw for a moment. There are a number of very strong muscles in that area. Just momentarily tense as many face muscles as you can, and then – relax. Allow your jaw muscles to loosen and let go. Notice how nice that feels.

Now let your attention wander to the rest of the muscles in your face. Allow your eye muscles to release, and let your cheeks and forehead relax.

Let this peaceful feeling flow slowly down your neck. Feel it sooth your throat and dissolve any tension as it slowly glides down to your shoulders.

Now momentarily tense your shoulders, squeeze them in and up. Now let your shoulders go. Give them a moment of your attention, and just mentally repeat the word "relax" as you let them soften, let go, and release all tension.

Allow that relaxed feeling to spill down your arms.

Now bring your awareness to your arms and tense them momentarily. Then let go. Feel them becoming loose and limp. They are relaxed and at peace, all the way from your shoulders, through your elbows, wrists, right to the tips of your fingers.

Now focus on the muscles in your back....all those muscles surrounding your spine. Tense all those muscles, and those around your tummy and ribcage, and then relax and let go.

Bring your awareness to your chest. Allow your breath to release this area. Imagine your breath whispering to your chest, 'relax'.

As you breathe in and out feel your stomach gently rise and fall. Let your stomach soften and relax with each breath. Feel it releasing tension as each moment passes. You can feel yourself slowly slipping into a state of deep relaxation.

Now bring your attention to your buttocks and thighs, tense them for a moment, then release. Imagine all those strong supporting muscles beginning to relax and unwind. Do the same with your knees ...your calves...your feet. Let them all relax.

Now just enjoy this relaxed feeling for a few moments. It does feel so good.

This relaxed feeling is yours. You have achieved it. Take a Mindful snapshot (an awareness snapshot) of it. Take it with you and bring it to mind throughout your day as you wish to.

Doing Things Mindfully

So what is being Mindful? Buddha advocated that one should maintain a calm awareness of oneself, our thoughts, our physical feelings and emotions as we interact with our environment, our circumstances. This awareness should be an attentive awareness and a truthful one.

It is worth exploring the concept of attentive and truthful awareness as therein lies the wisdom.

How often do we truly pay whole-hearted and whole-minded attention to 'I'? How often do we actually pay attention to how we are 'being'? Being doesn't just mean behaving; to be is to exist. Do we ever place our thoughts on our existence on purpose? What do you know about your own breathing? When do you pay attention to the multitude of tasks your body carries out automatically hundreds of times a day. How does your heart beating feel? Are you so caught up thinking 'I am stressed' or 'I am unwell' or 'I can't cope', that you never pay attention to what 'I' actually is and more to the point how 'I' actually feels. What we do rather is to identify our existence 'our self' as our thoughts. We believe we are what we are thinking and are actually mostly oblivious to what our existence really feels like, really is, in this very specific moment.

I invite you to think on this now. Whatever you are doing now – do it mindfully. 'I am reading' you may think. Pay attention to yourself reading. What are your eyes doing? What about your ears? How are you breathing? Are you warm? How do your clothes feel on your skin? Are you sitting or standing? What are your legs doing whilst you believe you are reading? Is reading really all you are doing? Are you sitting near a window and obliviously soaking up the sun? Is a bird singing, but you hadn't registered your ears hearing it? Is someone shouting in the distance, or an engine revving, and only now you realise your hands or legs or jaw have tensed in reaction to this?

For a few moments, don't read this book. Close your eyes, take a few deeper than normal breaths and then just place your attention on you, your breathing, your interaction with your immediate environment via all of your senses, touch, hearing, sight, smell, taste. For as many moments as you choose, place your conscious attention on you in this moment and begin to become aware of how 'now' actually is in your immediate existence. Allow yourself to realise you are, at a minimum, in so many ways - ok. How does being ok feel? What is purely existing like?

If you participated in that exercise, you have just been Mindful.

Very often in Mindfulness courses you are asked when home to do a normal everyday task, but to do it mindfully. It can be a task you enjoy or one you don't – it doesn't matter. On one such occasion I chose the washing up as my task. I need to set the scene as in 'washing up' was a task I had been doing with an immense level of disdain. Quite simply, I stated at that time 'I hate washing up'. In my perception it had become a relentless, never ending task. I would come home from long days at work, long days being 14 hour shifts, and feel greeted by the sight of washing up everywhere. Plates left on the couch, glasses on the window sills and coffee table. Saucepans and utensils in the kitchen. Even mugs on the bath side. Yes, you've guessed it – I had teenagers living at home. Teenagers who in my opinion weren't working and were required to spend relatively little time at college, and way too much time at home eating and drinking. And of course, they never used the same cup twice. The art of rinsing out a cup just did not exist in their world.

It had become a stress trigger - open door, see washing up, vroom!

So on this chosen occasion, I chose the task called washing up to do mindfully. I went around the house collecting the plates, bowls, cups, glasses. I paid attention to how I was feeling, what it was like to do this action. I was impressed by how many cups I could carry in one hand. I noticed how having long fingers really helped the process as I could carry three mugs using one finger by placing the finger though the handles. I filled the bowl with hot water, having squirted in some washing up liquid and watched the bubbles forming. I did this mindfully and it was really interesting watching the bubbles forming. And then I placed my hands in the bowl and that was decidedly pleasant. Warm water. As I washed the plates particularly, I noticed how satisfying it wash to wipe the 'stuff' off. And that moment you hold it up before placing it on the drainer, I became aware of. I have white plates and they sparkled. I realised that in actuality, there was a lot of enjoyment in washing up. I had simply never paid attention. It wasn't washing up that was the stress trigger, washing up had come to represent the stress and unhappiness I felt when I believed my children were inconsiderate despite my many attempts to address it.

What was accomplished by this exercise? I came to know the many 'its' for what they truly are. It is not the washing up I hate. I had conceptualised an emotion I had been evoking. Washing up came to represent the disappointment, the sadness I felt by my children's lack of action maybe? And then of course, I paid attention to those emotions, and worked out for the very first time that even they were my translation. Actually washing up came to represent the disappointment and sadness I felt because my expectations had not been met. My kids weren't cruel, they do care. They are inconsiderate – yes. They literally do not consider the emotional impact their carelessness, thoughtlessness, whatever word I wish to attach to their actions or lack of, evoke in me. Remember this is not a conversation about whether they should or shouldn't do it. This is me looking at my reaction to what currently is.

Furthermore, the habitual and excessive reaction I was having to opening the front door and seeing a dirty plate or cup, was totally unnecessary. Totally understandable maybe also. I did not beat myself up for feeling that way and I am sure it is usual to feel that way. But, were my reactions helpful in terms of either solving the situation or in terms of how I experienced coming in from work. I didn't have to notice the dirty plate or cup as soon as I walked in. I could have noticed a multitude of others things first, but I had become conditioned to notice that. I conditioned myself to notice that.

This is simply an example. However it is an example of the profound understanding of ourselves that comes from doing just ordinary everyday things mindfully.

It is unbelievable how preconditioned and judgemental and presumptuous we truly are. We cause ourselves immeasurable needless suffering. Simply life does not have to feel like this. Simply this is not how life is, it is how we are thinking it to be.

So from that point, in the next moment, yes the plates and cups are still there, but the thoughts and feelings I had attached to them aren't. The feelings of resentment, being unloved, being uncared about, being taken advantage of etc., etc., had never been the intention and they did not have to be result. I have a choice. I can choose to keep thinking and reacting that way if I feel there is a reason to or a benefit from. Neither Mindfulness nor being mindful makes any choices for me. It simply makes me aware of what actually is.

I choose not to suffer over washing up. I choose to continue to teach my children to be considerate and think in terms of potential cause and effect. I choose to continue to teach them to be clean and hygienic. But I do not suffer from things I erroneously believe to be facts anymore. And I now enjoy washing up.

How Does Mindfulness Help?

It is important from the beginning to realise that Mindfulness Practice will always be work in progress. There is no end result; it is about continuum.

To summarise, Mindfulness is about being aware of everyday life. Mindfulness does not avoid reality, rather it runs into it. It is a way of being, a way to live life.

Mindfulness develops acceptance and non-judgement; thus it reduces expectation, fear, resistance and pain and it increases fulfilment, fluidity and enjoyment. Becoming mindful widens our perspectives, it increases our awareness. It develops concentration and aids rest. It brings every part of life to life, because it brings real life to our attention. This is not our 'thought' life, it is real life.

Practising Mindfulness enables us to observe ourselves without judgement. It enables us to realise our self in this moment, as it is; no ribbons or bows, no devils or demons. It is not about how we should or should not be; it is about 'seeing me just as I am'. It develops compassion for 'me as I am' and by default then enables and facilitates compassion for all.

We become able to accept ourselves without judgment, so damaged self-esteem, self-sabotaging thoughts, avoidance and rumination all become alleviated.

Mindfulness teaches us how to observe, accept and choose, as opposed to grab or resist.

Life is a constant flow of one situation after another. In reality life is a continuous flow. Each event and circumstance changes moment by moment. One moment ultimately disintegrates into the next, this is unavoidable. We cannot grab hold of; we cannot resist. Life happens anyway, moving moment by moment, forever changing with each tick of the second hand.

So instead of ending up desperately trying to recreate a past circumstance, or desperately trying to avoid a potential future one, we learn to become aware of the flow, to watch, allow and accept and make use of what life brings. Instead of missing the majority of our own life, we become aware of it. Those devastating feelings of disappointment and failure fade as we kick out predetermined expectations and learn to see from a new perspective. This in turn alleviates thoughts and feelings that lead to depression.

We often feel that nothing goes the way we want it to, circumstance remains beyond our control, life swirls around us anyway, despite our desperate attempts, doing as it does. We try our best to control it, but we cannot control something that is forever moving, shifting and reshaping. We end up in mental chaos.

Mental culture reduces mental chaos. When we stop fighting and begin to accept that what is in this moment is in this moment, and see that it is neither good or bad, rather it simply is, but only in this moment, then we begin to calm down and really 'Come, See'.

For in each moment there is a multitude of things to see. Our life 'feels' like where we place our attention. Where our attention is, is where our experience of reality is. Suddenly we realise we are able to choose our existence from a multitude of choices, simply by choosing where to place our attention.

This Mindful mental state then impacts on our emotions because invariably, emotion follows thought. As we begin to think ok, we begin to feel ok.

Emotion in turn impacts on our physiology. Research has proven beyond doubt that every cell in our physical body reacts to our emotion. This is the reason Mindfulness is extremely useful in reducing the physical effects of stress and pain and illness.

'Existing mindfully' positively affects our interactions with our environment and with our fellow creatures. It changes our 'feel' for life, it gives us a choice of perspectives and experiences and therefore it actually changes our perception of reality. Mindfulness really does change our life.

Our very own life simply opens up as we really 'Come, See'.

Some Shared Experiences

Throughout the book I have shared some of my own experiences. I thought it would be good to have a section simply sharing some others.

The benefit of this is we begin to understand the vast applications of Mindfulness. We begin to see the many ways in which it can help, be it in work, play or healthcare.

The other benefit is to help you to truly know, if your experience is not as I have stated mine was, that does not mean you are doing it wrong.

++++++++

As a direct result of attending the Living in the Moment group, one service user relayed how it had helped her as an individual. It had been the case that this particular service user, at the time residing in a Secure Forensic Unit, had always found refusals from staff hard to cope with, particularly around leave requests. She explained 'hearing that no' would make her immediately feel angry. She 'felt' like she was being unfairly controlled and confined. As the relevant emotions surfaced with these thoughts, it would often occur that when her request was declined she would kick out, shouting obscenities, banging doors or tables, and her behaviour actually did more to ensure she was refused leave next time than it did to help her cause. An example of typical self-sabotaging behaviour, that was felt by her to be as uncontrollable as it was unhelpful and predictable by us.

Now however, she explained, when she went to request leave, she took the two deep breaths, thereby cueing the relaxed status which abated the predetermined anger, which in turn then gave her the chance to apply Mindfulness principles to the situation. This resulted in her being able to hold a reasonable and effective discussion with the staff, which since had resulted in them saying yes to her requests more often than not, as they observed and acknowledged her new found ability to control her own behaviours and reactions, (which was mainly the reason for the refusals of her requests in the first place).

In this lady's perspective, learning Mindfulness, got her leave requests accepted. In actuality it did far more than that as it gave her the ability to exist in a self-controlled and appropriate manner, which improved her own life in so many different situations.

Plus, the lady only had to take two deep breaths and her mind brought about the conditioned body state of relaxed; it took the cue and it works quickly.

++++++++

"I can accept myself and my illness. In fact, because I can accept myself, I don't see my illness (EUPD) as an illness anymore really."

++++++++

"My anxiety was at such a high level, I had stopped being able to go outside. Using Mindfulness techniques, I stopped fighting with my anxiety and got to know it. I realised that the symptoms were my brains way of making my body make me aware of danger. Of course there was no danger, but first I had to stop and get to know what was happening. Once I did that, I too realised of course there is no danger and the symptoms began subsiding all by themselves. They didn't totally go away immediately, but they definitely subsided enough for me to begin making a recovery."

++++++++

"I just see everything so differently now. I have stopped presuming other people think the same way I do. And I have definitely noticed now that what I am thinking isn't fact at all!"

++++++++

"I notice stuff now".

++++++++

"Regular meditation has brought a calmness to my life. Even when everything around me is frantic, I'm not. That has made a huge difference to my quality of life."

++++++++

"What mindfulness has done in me and with me after a diagnosis of cancer followed by chemotherapy has been like a new lease on life: Putting things into perspective, setting new priorities, appreciating little things. Yet, the most valuable practice has been to learn to live in the moment and not to get gripped by fear and unnecessary worry. I came to appreciate the truth that this would steal away too many hours, days, weeks and months of my life. Instead, I have learned to live by my new motto, enjoy life and living."

++++++++

I live with an active mind, thinking about the past and future, often worrying about what has happened or what might happen. I can miss the opportunity to be present – to be here and now.

++++++++

Mindfulness has changed my life. And it could do the same to yours. After five days in silence on a meditation course, I discovered an invaluable sense of stillness and calm, (24).

++++++++

I feel like science and spirituality just merged. I like it.

++++++++

Mindfulness is as it is. It began as a step on the road to finding peace. It remains the same now as it was then – so profound in its own simplicity. I hope I have stated its case in a helpful way. Mandy

<u>Glossary of Terms</u>

CBT – Cognitive Behavioural Therapy

DSM V - Diagnostic and Statistical Manual of Mental Disorders, Fifth Edition

FDA – US Food and Drug Agency. This agency approves the licensing of all new drugs licensed for use in the USA.

IAPTS – UK National Programme designed to improve access to psychological therapies.

ICD 10 – International Classification of Diseases

MBCT – Mindfulness Based Cognitive Therapy

MBSR – Mindfulness Based Stress Reduction

Mental Health Foundation - Mental Health Charity

NICE - National Institute for Health and Care Excellence - provides national guidance and advice to improve health and social care.

NLP – Neuro Linguistic Programming

NSAID – Non steroidal anti-inflammatory drug. Includes paracetamol, naproxen and many commonly used analgesics.

OCD – Obsessive Compulsive Disorder

PRN – Latin 'Pro re nata', the term given to medication prescribed for use when the circumstances warrant them. Whether the circumstances warrant them is the decision of the person giving the medication.

Time to Talk – UK Primary Care Service offering talking therapies.

Bibliography

1. **Gunaratana, Henepola.** *Mindfulness In Plain English.* West Virginia : H. Gunaratana Mahathera, 1990.

2. **Kabat-Zin, John.** *Full Catastrophe Living (Revised Edition).* London : Piatkus, Little Brown Book Company, 2013.

3. **Department of Health.** *No Health Without Mental Health: A cross Government mental health strategy for people of all ages. Supporting document – The economic.* s.l. : Department of Health, 2012.

4. **McCrone, P, et al.** *Paying The Price.* King's Fund. London : King's Fund, 2008. 978 1 857175 714.

5. **Mental Health Foundation.** Response to new research revealing a significant increase in anti-depressant prescriptions. *Mental Health Foundation.* [Online] 28th May 2014. [Cited: 26th June 2014.]

6. **Kirsch, I, et al.** Initial Severity and Antidepressant Benefits: A Meta-Analysis of Data Submitted to the Food and Drug Administration. *PLOS Medicine.* [Online] 26th February 2008. [Cited: 8th July 2014.] http://www.plosmedicine.org/article/info:doi/10.1371/journal .pmed.0050045.

7. **National Institute for Health and Care Excellence.** Anxiety disorders. *National Institute for Health and Care Excellence.* [Online] 2014 National Institute for Health and Care Excellence., February 2014. [Cited: 3rd March 2015.] https://www.nice.org.uk/guidance/qs53.

8. **—.** Generalised Anxiety Disorder. *National Institute for Health and Care Excellence.* [Online] National Institute for Health and Care Excellence, March 2012. [Cited: 7th July

2014.] http://pathways.nice.org.uk/pathways/generalised-anxiety-disorder?fno=1#content=view-quality-statement%3Aquality-statements-pharmacological-treatment&path=view%3A/pathways/generalised-anxiety-disorder/step-3-gad-with-marked-functional-impairment-or-that-h.

9. **Patient.co.uk.** Benzodiazepines and Z Drugs. *Patient.co.uk.* [Online] Egton Medical Information Systems Limited, 27th November 2013. [Cited: 7th July 2014.] http://www.patient.co.uk/health/benzodiazepines-and-z-drugs.

10. **Royal College of Psychiatrists.** Benzodiazepines. *RC Psych.* [Online] The Royal College of Psychiatrists, July 2013. [Cited: 3rd March 2015.] http://www.rcpsych.ac.uk/healthadvice/treatmentswellbeing/benzodiazepines.aspx.

11. **Szasz MD, Thomas S.** *The Myth of Mental Illness.* New York : Harper Perennial, 2010. 978-0-06-177122-4.

12. **Shorter, E.** *Before Prozac.* New York : Oxford University Press, 2009. 978-0-19-536874-1 .

13. **Moncrieff, Dr Joanna.** Books, papers and blogs by Joanna Moncrieff. *Joanna Moncrieff.* [Online] [Cited: 16th March 2015.] http://joannamoncrieff.com/papers/.

14. **Personnel Today.** How practising mindfulness in the workplace can boost productivity. *Occupational Health.* [Online] Reed Business Information Ltd, 1st May 2013. [Cited: 3rd March 2015.] http://www.personneltoday.com/hr/how-practising-mindfulness-in-the-workplace-can-boost-productivity/.

15. **Baugh, Barbara.** Health Psychology Homepage: Electroconvulsive Therapy and Depression. *Vanderbilt*

University. [Online] David Schlundt, PhD, 4th October 2009. [Cited: 3rd March 2015.] http://healthpsych.psy.vanderbilt.edu/2009/ECT_Depression. htm.

16. **Nicholson, A.** *Oh Why Did I Do That!? ... and what to do about it.* London : Esteem World Publications, 2013.

17. **Andreassi, John L.** *Psychophysiology. Human Behaviour and Physiological Response.* Fifth Edition. Mahwah, New Jersey, London : Lawrence Earlbaum Associates, 2007. 0 8058 4951 3.

18. **Hicks, E and Hicks, J.** *The 'Astonishing Power of Emotions - Let Your Feelings Be Your Guide.* London : Hay House UK Ltd, 2007. 978 1 4019 1577 3 .

19. **Mann, D.** Even Mild Dehydration May Cause Emotional, Physical Problems. *WebMD.* [Online] 20th January 2012. [Cited: 8th July 2014.] http://www.webmd.com/women/news/20120120/even-mild-dehydration-may-cause-emotional-physical-problems.

20. **Prince of Wales International Centre.** MBCT. *minfulness based cognitive therapy.* [Online] Prince of Wales International Centre. [Cited: 19th March 2015.] http://mbct.co.uk/.

21. **National Institute for Health and Care Excellence.** NICE Evidence Search - Mindfulness. *NICE.* [Online] National Institute for Health and Care Excellence, 2014. [Cited: 9th July 2014.] https://www.evidence.nhs.uk/search?q=Mindfulness.

22. **Hall Ph.D, Nick.** I Know What To Do, So Why Don't I Do It? [prod.] Dave Kuenstle. *I Know What To Do, So Why Don't I Do It?* [CD] Paignton : Nightingale Conant.

23. **O'Connor, Joseph.** *NLP Workbook.* Berwick upon Tweed : Thorsons, 2002.

24. **Lennox, Anthony Gordon.** Mindfulness has changed my life. And it could do the same to yours. *The Telegraph.* [Online] Telegraph Media Group Limited 2015, 19th March 2015. [Cited: 19th March 2015.] http://www.telegraph.co.uk/comment/10819646/Mindfulnes s-has-changed-my-life.-And-it-could-do-the-same-to-yours.html.

25. **Mental Health Foundation.** Mental Health Statistics. *Mental Health Foundation.* [Online] June 2014. [Cited: 26th June 2014.] http://www.mentalhealth.org.uk/help-information/mental-health-statistics/anxiety-statistics/?view=Standard.

About the Author

Amanda Nicholson BSc RNMH, or Mandy as she prefers to be called, is a Registered and practising Mental Health Nurse and Author.

Mandy obtained her Bachelor of Science (Hons) degree at University of Surrey, Guildford, England. She has also studied NLP and Mindfulness Practice.

Mandy published her first book 'Oh Why Did I Do That!? ... and what to do about it' in June 2013. A revised edition was published in April 2014. This book has received excellent reviews from a variety of sectors.

Mandy has worked in many physical and mental healthcare settings. She initiated a successful Living In The Moment Group in a Secure and Forensic setting and was involved in applied Mindfulness as a Nursing Approach in an Acute Inpatient Setting. She co-presents an Introduction to Mindfulness Course for the Community Recovery College. She continues to write material for Mindfulness in the Workplace.

Mandy has personally practised Mindfulness in excess of 20 years, or as she says, 'before I knew it was called Mindfulness'.

Coming from an executive background as a Financial Controller, Mandy is well placed for her latest Mindfulness venture of integrating Mindfulness as a working, commercial project, incorporating the topical 'Mindfulness in the Workplace' and 'Mindful Management'.

Oh Why Did I Do That!? ... and what to do about it.

By Amanda Nicholson

How many times do we ask 'Oh Why Did I Do That? There are valid reasons for the things we do. Stop beating yourself up, start understanding those reasons, then start appreciating you. From that point of understanding you can begin to do, feel and think how you want to. Become the master of you instead of the victim.

• Halt those habitual responses and make an informed choice.

• Learn how to see things from different perspectives in each moment

• Challenge the judgments and beliefs that are limiting your experience.

• Learn how to stay well and have fun.

Physiology and Mindfulness combine to provide a practical and holistic solution to the question 'Oh Why Did I Do That?'

Reviews – Oh Why Did I Do That!? ... and what to do about it.

Real Life Mindful Practices for a Calm and Less Stressed Life! The author knows what she is talking about. This explains mindfulness and how it can be brought into everyday life. It is something we all can do – something that can change our reactions and beliefs.

PL Verified Amazon Purchase (CT USA)

In Mandy Nicholson's 'Oh why did I do that!?...and what to do about it' key elements of developmental and behavioural psychology, neurophysiology and linguistics are interwoven from an informed first person perspective to present mindfulness in a readily understandable and practicable format. Mandy is a naturally confident narrator who writes with motivation and an immediacy and clarity that both fascinates and informs as it inspires. This book is designed to help you develop a more positive and successful attitude towards yourself and your life by rethinking what does and doesn't work for you in the mindfulness context of acknowledgement and acceptance. The author has the self-insight, emotional intelligence and literary skill to make this a self-help book that does what it says; helps you to help yourself. This is definitely a book that I will benefit from rereading again and again.

SM – Doctor of Applied Mathematics

This book tells you a lot about yourself! I usually struggle with 'self-help' books, but this one gave plenty of insight into why we do things and gives tips and help in avoiding similar things happening in the future, without being 'too deep' and (for me) boring. I read the whole book in one evening and would certainly recommend it to a friend.

TJC - Aviation Historian

It's about options – and enables the reader to choose the options that help them help themselves – simple, easy to read and a gem of a book.

BB – Life Coach

I'm fairly new to working in a mental health setting and wanted a book to tell me about mindfulness in a hurry to get up to speed quickly. This book does that. It's like sitting down with the author whiles she says, this is what it is... It provides a grounding in mindfulness and enabled me to move on to Jon Kabat-Zin's book with confidence.

LT-Senior Occupational Therapist

I really enjoyed reading this book as it explains everything so clearly. It enables the reader to fully understand why things happen in regards to actions, thoughts and feelings. Backed up by research, this book can help you move forward in your life and get over obstacles that are in your mind's way. One of the things in this book that has stuck with me is: "When we hold a belief about ourselves that we do believe to be factual, we presume others hold the same belief." The realisation that we are not dictated to by our mind is wonderful. It has enabled me to go forward.

JOK – Marketing Consultant

Great book. Very informative and not too long. Excellent advice and information, especially for those of us who keep getting annoyed with ourselves! And it's written by a British lady which meant I could relate to it. Sometimes I find American self-help books a bit grating. This one is sensible and at times humorous.

MM - Verified Amazon Purchase (UK)